QUESTIONS ON THE THEORY OF CATERING

Ronald Kinton BEd(Hons), FHCIMA

*Formerly of
Garnett College, College of Education
for Teachers in Further and Higher Education*

Victor Ceserani MBE, MBA, FHCIMA

*Formerly Head of
The School of Hotelkeeping and Catering,
Ealing College of Higher Education*

To accompany *The Theory of Catering* sixth edition

Edward Arnold

A division of Hodder & Stoughton

LONDON   MELBOURNE   AUCKLAND

© Ronald Kinton and Victor Ceserani 1989

First published in Great Britain 1978
Second edition 1984
This edition 1989

British Library Cataloguing in Publication Data
Kinton, Ronald
  Questions on the theory of catering.
  1. Great Britain.   Catering
  I. Title   II. Ceserani, Victor
  647′.9541

  ISBN 0–340–49654–1

Typeset in Great Britain by Wearside Tradespools, Fulwell,
Sunderland
Printed and bound in Great Britain for Edward Arnold, the
educational, academic and medical publishing division of Hodder and
Stoughton Limited, Mill Road, Dunton Green, Sevenoaks, Kent by
Richard Clay Ltd, Bungay, Suffolk

Contents

Introduction

The aim of this workbook is to assist catering students in their revision by providing questions drawn from the 6th edition of *The Theory of Catering*. Students may work from the book on their own to test the effectiveness of their study of *The Theory of Catering*, and their own general knowledge of the subject. The questions should be answered from memory, from the student's own deductions or by reference to *The Theory of Catering*. It is the authors' opinion that revision by systematic use of this book throughout the course will result in a better knowledge of catering.

Many multiple choice questions are included and the book will be particularly useful for students taking City & Guilds of London Institute Catering examinations 705, 706/1 and 706/2, also BTEC Catering courses and the examinations of the HCIMA.

At the beginning of each chapter or sub-chapter are the numbers of the pages in *The Theory of Catering* (6th edition) where the answers may be found.

1

Food and society

pages 1–7

1 Briefly describe three factors which affect what we eat.

1

2

3

2 State three ways in which eating can develop social relationships.

1

2

3

3 State *your* food preferences and suggest where you think they originated.

4 List eight varied types of eating establishment.

1   2   3

4   5   6

7   8

5 Explain the difference between a *vegan* and a *vegetarian*.

6 Pair the following:

☐ historical	1 Chinese restaurant
☐ religious	2 health restaurant
☐ geographical	3 a fast (refrain from eating)
☐ physiological	4 fish and chip shop
☐ economic	5 wedding breakfast
☐ sociological	6 medieval banquet

7 Why in the 1950s did shops begin to turn to self-service?

8 Suggest two reasons why Chinese restaurants began to be popular in the 1950s.

1

2

9 Approximately what fraction of the population of Britain was poor and undernourished in Edwardian England?

☐ ⅛   ☐ ¼   ☐ ⅓   ☐ ⅙

10 Place in chronological order:

☐ Milk bars become the 'in-thing'
☐ Healthy eating becomes fashionable
☐ Co-operative societies develop
☐ Effective rationing occurs
☐ Tea shops at their peak

11 Which of the following have affected our eating habits?

☐ air transport	☐ food preservatives
☐ microwave ovens	☐ tourism
☐ supermarkets	☐ additives

12 Differentiate between a *gourmet* and a *gourmand*.

13 In the 1980s *nouvelle cuisine* became fashionable, but this has tended to give way to _____.

2

Influences of ethnic culture

pages 8–20

1 Give three reasons why it is essential to have a knowledge of ethnic cookery.

1

2

3

2 State four causes that have contributed to the increase in ethnic eating places.

1

2

3

4

3 Match the following:

☐ Muslims   1 Vesak
☐ Hindus   2 Ramadan
☐ Sikhs   3 Holi
☐ Buddhists   4 Baisakh day

4 Briefly explain in relation to food:

1 taboo

2 ethnic

3 gastronomy

4 physiological

5 kosher

6 additives

5 Match the following:

☐ hot cross buns   1 6th January
☐ crown cake   2 Good Friday
☐ pumpkin pie   3 Lent
☐ pancakes   4 Thanksgiving Day

6 Strict Jews eat only:

☐ minced meat   ☐ meat balls
☐ koshered meat   ☐ meat from goat

7 The Jewish plaited bread eaten on the Sabbath is called c_____

     – unleavened bread served at Passover is called m_____

     – a traditional dish served at Pentecost is c_____

8 Couscous is made from:

☐ barley   ☐ rice
☐ wheat   ☐ maize

9 Which is the odd one out?

☐ Chollah   ☐ Chapati
☐ Cerviche   ☐ Tortilla

10 What have the following in common?

Sushi   *Condé*

11 Match the following items with their country of origin:

☐ Goulash	1 Switzerland
☐ Lava bread	2 Greece
☐ Colcannon	3 America
☐ Bouillabaisse	4 Italy
☐ Haggis	5 Russia
☐ Gnocchi	6 Hungary
☐ Sauerkraut	7 Mexico
☐ Coulibiac	8 Japan
☐ Rösti	9 India
☐ Paella	10 France
☐ Taramasalata	11 Scotland
☐ Succotash	12 Ireland
☐ Guacamole	13 Wales
☐ Dim Sum	14 China
☐ Tofu	15 Spain

12 Waterchestnuts are used in the cookery of:

☐ Germany   ☐ India

☐ China   ☐ Mexico

3

The catering industry

pages 21–35

1 The economic health of a nation is reflected by _____ served in the home and in _____.

2 What special food requirements should be considered for old people with poor digestion?

3 Suggest three reasons for your answer to Q2.

1

2

3

4 Give a brief description of:

1 chain-catering organisations

2 welfare catering

5 In hospital a patient's treatment consists of:

1 skilled medical attention   2 careful nursing

3 _____

6 List four responsibilities of a dietitian in a hospital.

1   2

3   4

7 Give three different examples of residential establishments in the welfare sector.

1   2   3

8 The head office of many large companies provide luncheon _____ for their employees.

9 Give three different examples of transport catering.

1   2   3

10 Briefly explain what you understand by *contract catering*.

4

Menu planning

pages 36–81

1   What are the two functions of a menu?

    1

    2

2   Give two ways in which a caterer can be guilty of an offence under the Trade Descriptions Act.

    1

    2

3   The Trade Descriptions Act is concerned with:

    ☐ a clear account of the trade practised
    ☐ an accurate description of the item offered for sale
    ☐ a description of the various jobs in the trade
    ☐ an accurate account of the trades union

4   If 'eggs and bacon' were stated on the menu, should one or more than one egg be served?

5   It would be a contravention of the Trade Description Act to write on the menu 'fillet of haddock' and serve fillet of cod: true/false.

6   What is the main difference between a *table d'hôte* and an *à la carte* menu?

7 Would you consider cheese soufflé and grilled steak suitable items for a large banquet? Give reasons for your answer.

8 When are menu cards usually given to hospital patients?

9 Suggest three reasons why it is in the interest of progressive companies to offer a good catering service for their employees?

1

2

3

10 Name two important factors that should be considered when preparing meals for school children.

1   2

11 What is a *cyclical menu*?

12 Give two advantages and two disadvantages of cyclical menus?

1   2

1   2

13 The availability of both the _____ and _____

_____ must be considered when planning a menu.

14 The aim of menu planning is to give customers what they want, not what the caterer thinks they want: true/false.

15 The traditional name given to a set menu at a set price is:

☐ à la carte
☐ chef's selection
☐ meal of the day
✓☐ table d'hôte

16 An *à la carte* menu is one:

☐ for customers wanting a set menu
☐ where it is served from a buffet or cart
✓ ☐ where the dishes are individually priced
☐ used at a call order unit

17 State six important points that should be taken into consideration before planning a menu.

1

2

3

4

5

6

18 Give two reasons why it is sensible to use foods in season.

1

2

19 What are the dangers of planning menus without giving consideration to the kitchen equipment available?

20 Why should the capabilities of the serving staff be considered when selecting the dishes and plates on which food is served?

21 What is understood by *menu balance*?

22 Criticise the following menus:

1 Mushroom Soup
  Fillets of Sole Bonne Femme
  Boiled Chicken and Rice
  Mushroom and Bacon Savoury

2 Crème Portugaise
  Fillets of Sole Dugléré
  Hungarian Goulash
  Marquise Potatoes
  Stuffed Tomatoes
  Strawberry Flan

3 Potato Soup
  Fricassée of Veal
  Buttered Turnips
  Creamed Potatoes
  Meringue and Vanilla Ice-cream

23 State six common faults in menu planning.

1   2

3   4

5   6

24 What do you understand by *plate appeal*?

25 Give two examples of plated foods to illustrate your answer to the previous question.

1   2

26 Arrange in numerical order:

sept, un, dix, huit, trois, quatre, neuf, deux, six, cinq

27 Correct the four spelling errors in the following:

Le darne de saumon

La tronçon du turbot

Le selle d'agneau

La gigot d'agneau

28 *Farcir* means to fry: true/false.

11

29 Which is correct?

☐ le homard   ☐ la homard   ☐ l'homard

30 Add as appropriate le, la, les:

darne	selle	goujons
tronçon	coeur	gigot

31 Tick the correct one:

☐ le fillet de sole frits   ☐ les filet de sole frits
☐ la fillet de sole frit   ☐ les filets de sole frit

32 Correct the following:

farçi	entremetier
beure	crepes
persilees	choufleur
rôtisier	troson

33 Lemon pancakes written in French would be:

☐ crépes à le citron
☐ crêpes aux citron
☐ crêpes au citron
☐ crêpes au citrons

34 Correct the four spelling errors:

Consomé en tasse

Sole en gujons

Fillet de boeuf

Carrotes Vichy

35 Give the French for:

Apple tart

Lobster soup

Peas French style

Mashed potatoes

Banana fritters

Ham omelet

36 What do the following mean?

1 assaisoner

2 braiser

3 chauffer

4 concasser

37 *Mélanger* means:

☐ to mix   ☐ to emulsify
☐ to muddle   ☐ to make

38 Match the following:

☐ au four   1 scrambled
☐ les blancs d'oeufs   2 studded
☐ au vin blanc   3 cooked in the oven
☐ brouillé   4 a cooking liquid
☐ le court bouillon   5 mixed
☐ jus rôti   6 fixed price meal
☐ napper   7 egg whites
☐ clouté   8 gravy
☐ panaché   9 with white wine
☐ table d'hôte   10 to mask

39 *Paner* means:

☐ to pass through a sieve   ☐ to plate
☐ to pound   ✓ ☐ to egg and crumb

40 A *poche* is a :

☐ a pocket   ☐ an egg poaching pan
☐ a piping tube   ☐ a piping bag

41 Translate the following into French:

1 bread   2 bacon

3 butter   4 cheese

42 Translate the following into English:

1 l'oeuf   2 le jambon

3 la farine   4 le lait

43 Translate the following in to French:

1 lamb   2 pork

3 beef   4 veal

44 Translate the following into English:

1 le poulet   2 la dinde

3 le canard   4 le faisan

45 Complete the French names:

Brussels sprouts	les c_____	de B_____
Cauliflower	le c_____	f_____
French beans	les h_____	v_____
Mushrooms	les c_____	

46 Complete the French names:

Apple	la _____
Banana	la _____
Cherry	la _____
Lemon	le _____
Orange	l' _____
Pear	la_____
Pineapple	l' _____

47 *Brunoise* means:

☐ small neat dice   ☐ braising
☐ basic brown sauce   ☐ browning

48 *Contrefilet* is a:

☐ large fillet steak   ☐ boned wing rib of beef
☐ small fillet steak   ☐ boned sirloin of beef

49 *Navarin* is a:

☐ navy dish of pork and beans   ☐ Normandy speciality of tripe
☐ brown lamb or mutton stew   ☐ Northern France pancake

50 *Ragoût* means:

☐ grill   ☐ stew

☐ boil   ☐ fried

51 Translate this menu into French:

Watercress soup

Fried cod with tomato sauce

Chips

Apple pie

52 Which is correct?

☐ hors-d'oeuvres variés   ☐ hor-d'oeuvres varié

☐ hor-d'oeuvre variés   ☑ hors-d'oeuvre variés

53 Match the following:

☐ la louche	1 frying pan
☐ la poche	2 bacon
☐ la poêle	3 loin
☑ le lard	4 ladle
☐ la longe	5 conical strainer
☑ le chinois	6 piping bag

54 Which would be served as a sweet dish and which as a meat dish?

Le riz -> sweet ·

Le ris -> meat ·

55 Translate the following into French:

Cod

Whitebait

Haddock

Oyster

Prawn

56 Write the following in French suitable for a menu:

 Stuffed loin of lamb

 Grilled lamb chop

 Liver and bacon

 Braised duck with peas

 Jugged hare

 Cauliflower soup

 Leaf spinach

 Cherry tartlet

57 If the house policy is to write all menus in English what would you do with:

 1 mayonnaise

 2 hors-d'oeuvre

 3 consommé

58 Poulet Sauté Parmentier has a garnish of:

 ☐ turned potatoes
 ☐ duchesse potatoes
 ☐ 1 cm dice potatoes
 ☐ sauté potatoes

59 Compile a four course menu illustrating good balance of texture, food value, colour etc.

60 Which way do you prefer to see this item on the menu? Give your reason why:

 ☐ Poched Turbot with Hollandaise Sauce
 ☐ Sea fresh succulent Turbot with Dutch butter sauce
 ☐ Turbot Poché Sauce Hollandaise
 ☐ Turbot Poché Sauce Hollandaise (Boiled Turbot and Hollandaise Sauce)

61 Match these items:

☐ Condé	1 coffee
☐ Washington	2 tomatoes
☐ Véronique	3 sweetcorn
☐ Doria	4 cucumber
☐ Mornay	5 cauliflower
☐ Portugaise	6 cheese
☐ Moka	7 rice
☐ Dubarry	8 grapes

62 Truite meunière Bretonne is shallow fried trout garnished with:

☐ capers and lemon segments
☐ turned pieces of cucumber
☐ soft roes, mushrooms and tomato
☑ shrimps and sliced mushrooms

63 What flavour would *Suchard* indicate on the menu?

chocolate

64 Praliné ice-cream would contain what ingredient?

praline.

65 In sweet dishes what ingredient is indicated by these terms?

1 Chantilly

2 Normande

3 Montmorency

4 Melba

5 Hélène

66 What ingredient is indicated by the use of these words?

1 Clamart

2 Lyonnaise

3 Florentine

4 Princesse

67 What is the difference between a traditional English breakfast and a continental breakfast?

68 List three points to consider when compiling a breakfast menu.

1

2

3

69 At which meal would these dishes most likely be served? Indicate B for breakfast, L for lunch and D for dinner.

☐ egg and bacon   ☐ rice pudding
☐ boiled beef and carrots   ☐ kipper
☐ treacle pudding   ☐ sorbet
☐ suprême de volaille   ☐ liver and bacon

70 Suggest three first courses suitable for the lunch menu in a medium priced hotel in summer.

1

2

3

71 Would these dishes usually be offered for luncheon or dinner?

braised oxtail   braised sweetbreads

steak and kidney pudding   Irish stew

chicken casserole   hot pot

72 Suggest three light English sweets suitable for a worker's canteen menu in summer.

1   2   3

73 Suggest a typical three course English luncheon menu for a party of overseas visitors on their first visit to England.

74 The party in the previous question who had an early breakfast and a light lunch, require a real English tea. What would you offer them?

75 Suggest eight suitable items for a dish of French pastries.

1   2

3   4

5   6

7   8

76 Name four popular items that may be served toasted for tea.

1   2

3   4

77 Suggest three interesting first courses for dinner at a commercial hotel in winter.

1   2   3

78 Indicate the fish which are more suitable for dinner menus than lunch menus?

☐ cod   ☐ sole
☐ herring   ☐ salmon trout

79 A sorbet is a:

☐ type of sauce   ☐ lightly frozen water ice
☐ type of vegetable   ☐ a double sized sausage

80 Suggest three interesting sweets suitable for hospital patients on a normal diet in winter.

1   2   3

81 Suggest a four course dinner menu for 24 very important people to be served in November with no expense spared.

82 In April the office block annual party for 100 people requires a light supper at 11 pm. What would you offer them?

83 Match these items:

☐ entrée   1 macaroni au gratin
☐ roast   2 vol-au-vent
☐ savoury   3 egg mayonnaise
☐ farinaceous   4 Welsh rarebit
☐ hors-d'oeuvre   5 best end of lamb

84 On which courses of the menu would these dishes be placed?

Cheese soufflé

Raised pie

Whitebait

Camembert

Potted shrimps

85 State two important points to be considered when compiling a banquet menu.

1

2

86 Why should heavily garnished dishes be avoided for banquets?

87 Can banquets be offered for both luncheon and dinner? yes/no.

88 Name four different types of buffet.

1   2

3   4

89 Suggest a menu for one of the buffets named in the previous answer, for 250 people at Christmas in a moderately priced seaside hotel.

90 What is an essential requirement for food prepared for a fork buffet?

91 It is usual to serve canapés as one of the varieties of foods at cocktail parties: true/false.

92 Suggest six interesting canapés.

1   2

3   4

5   6

93 What size should canapés be?

94 Name six items of a savoury nature suitable for a buffet.

1   2

3   4

5   6

5

Commodities

1 Meat

pages 83–96

1 Why is it necessary to know and understand the structure of meat in order to cook it properly?

2 Lean flesh is composed of m_____ which are numerous bundles of f_____ held together by connective tissue.

3 The size of fibres in meat affects the grain and texture of the meat: true/false.

4 There are two kinds of connective tissue, the yellow e____ _____ and the white c_____.

5 The quantity of connective tissue that binds the fibres together has much to do with the tenderness and eating quality of the meat: true/false

6 As the yellow connective tissue will not cook, how must it be dealt with?

7 When the white connective tissue is cooked it decomposes in moist heat to form g_____.

8   The quantity and quality of fat are important factors in determining eating quality of meat: true/false.

9   Briefly discuss the previous question.

10 Meat is hung to:
    ☐ increase leanness
    ☐ enable the blood to congeal
    ☐ increase the flavour and tenderness
    ☐ facilitate jointing

11 Briefly discuss your answer to the previous question.

12 Meat is generally hung at a temperature of
    ☐ −1°C   ☐ 1°C   ☐ 2°C   ☐ 4°C

13 Match the following:
    ☐ pig   1 lamb and mutton
    ☐ calf   2 pork and bacon
    ☐ sheep   3 veal

14 *La viande* is French for _____.

15 List four points to consider when storing fresh meat.
    1   2

    3   4

16 List four points to consider when storing fresh bacon.
    1   2

    3   4

17 Describe how you would recognise good quality beef.

18   Are supplies of home produced veal obtainable all year round? yes/no.

19   The quality of veal necessary for first class cookery requires a carcass of meat weighing approximately 100 kg: true/false.

20   Would veal described as pale pink, firm and moist with firm pinkish white fat be of good or poor quality?

21   Could Britain be called a lamb eating country?

22   Although in Britain we produce much of our own lamb and mutton, from which other country do we import large quantities?

23   *Lamb* is the term given to animals not more than:
     ☐ 1 year old   ☐ 1½ years old
     ☐ 2 years old   ☐ 3 years old

24   Good quality lamb should have:
     ☐ lean, firm, bright red, fine grain flesh; hard, white, evenly distributed fat.
     ☐ lean, soft, bright red, fine grain flesh; hard, white, evenly distributed fat.
     ☐ lean, soft, dull red, fine grain flesh; hard, white, evenly distributed fat.
     ☐ lean, firm, dull red, fine grain flesh; hard, white, evenly distributed fat.

25   Pork must always be well cooked because:
     ☐ otherwise it will be greasy and tasteless
     ☐ that is the way customers like it
     ☐ otherwise it will be tough and stringy
     ☐ *trichinae* (parasitic worms) may be present and must be destroyed by heat

26   Briefly describe good quality pork.

27 Briefly describe the two methods of curing bacon.

1

2

28 Green bacon has a milder flavour than smoked bacon: true/false.

29 *Bacon* is the cured flesh of the baconer pig: true/false.

30 *Ham* is the hind leg of:
☐ porker pig, cut square, pickled, dried and smoked
☐ baconer pig, cut square, pickled, dried and smoked
☐ porker pig, cut round with the aitchbone, pickled, dried and smoked
☐ baconer pig, cut round with the aitchbone, pickled, dried and smoked

31 All hams must be well cooked before being eaten: true/false.

32 What is the food value of meat?

33 List four ways of preserving meat.

1   2

3   4

34 What is meant by *chilled meat*?

35 Which one of the diagrams below is correct according to the key?

1 ☐   2 ☐   3 ☐   4 ☐

A leg	E shoulder
B breast	F scrag end
C middle neck	G best end
D saddle	

36 When ordering *prepared beef* from the butcher, what would be supplied if you ordered:

1 striploin

2 pony

3 rib-eye roll

37 What is the difference between a *full* and a *short baron* of beef?

38 Briefly describe:

1 haunch of veal

2 chine and end of veal

3 escalopes of veal

4 veal steaks

39 A prepared single chine and end of veal is called _____?

40 What would the butcher supply if you ordered:

1 rack of lamb

2 hind of lamb

3 crown of lamb

41 Cuts across an uncut pair of best ends would produce _____?

42 With pork, what is the difference between a *long* and a *short hogmeat*?

43 A suckling pig usually weights:

☐ 6–8 lbs   ☐ 8–10 lbs
☐ 10–20 lbs   ☐ 20–22 lbs

44 the spare rib of pork is part of:

☐ long loin
☐ short loin
☐ neck-end
☐ middle hogmeat

2   Offal

pages 97–100

1 The edible parts taken from the inside of the carcass are called:

2 State the names of four items referred to in the previous question.

1   2   3   4

3 *Tripe* is the _____ lining or white _____ of the ox.

4 The best tripe is:

☐ Honeydew   ☐ Velvet
☐ Honeycomb   ☐ Smooth

5 Oxtails should be of good size, meaty and lean: true/false.

6 Give one use of each of the following:

1 sheep's head

2 calf's head

3 pig's head

7 Give three quality points and one use for beef suet:

1

2

3

Use

8 From where is beef marrow obtained?

9 Name one use for each of the following:
1 lamb's kidney

2 calf's kidney

3 sheep's kidney

4 ox kidney

5 pig's kidney

10 The food value of kidney is similar to liver: true/false.

11 The hearts of which two animals are sometimes used in cookery?
1   2

12 The tongue of which animal is popular both as a hot and cold meat?

13 Ox-tongues must be salted before being used: true/false.

14 *Sweetbreads* are:

☐ glands which when cooked are nutritious and digestible
☐ small balls of stuffing served with chicken
☐ offal obtained from suckling pigs
☐ glands from the pancreas and heart used for diets
☐ sweet tasting stomach lining

15 Heart sweetbreads are superior in quality to the neck sweetbreads: true/false.

3 Poultry

pages 100–103

1 *Poultry* is the term which covers:

☐ domestic birds which are free ranging
☐ edible domestic birds and wild birds
☐ edible birds which have finished laying
☐ domestic birds bred to be eaten

2 Indicate the correct poultry quality points:

☐ The bird's breast should be plump
☐ The flesh should be firm
☐ The vent-end of the breastbone must be pliable
☐ The skin should be white and unbroken
☐ Young birds have spurs and large scales on their legs

3 The flesh of poultry is more easily digested than that of butcher's meat: true/false.

4 Unlike meat, fresh poultry need not be hung: true/false.

5 Frozen birds must be kept in the deep freeze unit until required to be defrosted: true/false.

6 When defrosting birds it is best to:

☐ place them in warm water
☐ place them in cold water
☐ place them on the kitchen table
☐ place them in the refrigerator

7   Match the following:

□ Baby (spring) chicken   1 Broiler
□ Capon   2 Old hen
□ Boiling fowl   3 4–6 weeks old
□ Medium roasting chicken   4 Large roasting bird

8   The smallest chicken is known as a _____.

9   The largest chicken is known as a _____.

10 Put in order of size – smallest first:

□ Turkey   □ Duck   □ Quail   □ Poussin

11 Turkeys are available in weights from _____ to _____.

12 Give three quality points for prime turkey.

1

2

3

13 What is grey and white, feathered and resembles a chicken?

14 What does *eviscerated* mean?

□ plucked
□ degutted
□ frozen
□ portioned

15 Chickens fed on maize are known as:

□ corn-fed
□ maize-fed
□ cereal-fed
□ range-fed

4 Game

pages 103–106

1 State five points to look for in quality of game birds.

   1   2

   3   4

   5

2 What do you understand by the term *game?*

3 Name the two groups into which game can be divided.

   1   2

4 Is game less or more fat than poultry or meat?

5 Game is easily digested: true/false.

6 Game birds and game animals are hung with their fur/feathers on: true/false.

7 Game must be hung to enable it to become _____ and to develop _____.

8 What are the four factors that determine the hanging time for game?

   1 t _____

   2 c _____

   3 a _____

   4 s _____ t _____

9 Place the following in order of size – smallest first.

   ☐ Wild duck   ☐ Pheasant   ☐ Partridge
   ☐ Grouse   ☐ Woodcock   ☐ Wood pigeon

10   What is the name given to the flesh of deer?

11   Give two quality points for joints of venison.

1 Well f _____

2 Dark b _____ r _____ colour

12   *Venison* is:

☐ old veal
☐ a type of paté
☐ a type of Scottish beef
☐ the flesh of deer

13   Why is venison marinaded before being cooked?

☐ To kill parasites
☐ To help its keeping quality
☐ To counteract toughness and dryness
☐ To form the base of the gravy

14   Of what significance are the ears of hares and rabbits?

15   What two kinds of rabbits are used for cooking?

16   With what are woodcock and snipe trussed?

5   Fish

pages 106–122

1   Which is the odd one out and why?

☐ haddock   ☒ herring   ☐ cod
☐ whiting   ☐ hake

others white fish - herring oily.

2   What have the following in common?

plaice   brill   sole   turbot   dab

what white, flat, fish

3 The approximate loss from boning and waste in the preparation of flat fish fillets is:

☐ 10%   ☐ 20%   ☐ 30%   ☑ 50%

4 The approximate loss from boning and waste in the preparation of round fish fillets is:

☑ 60%   ☐ 40%   ☐ 20%   ☐ 10%

5 Halibut and cod liver contain _vit. A + D_ .

6 State six points to be observed when purchasing fish.

1 Smell must be pleasant.   2 eyes, bright + full.

3 gills: 4 flesh - firm.

5 Scales, life flat, moist   6 skin - fresh, sea slime.
         bent out:

7 Which vitamins are contained in fish?

In oily fish especially, vit. A + D

8 Indicate the fish below using the following key: 'O' for oily or 'W' for white fish; 'F' for flat or 'R' for round fish.

☑ ☑ eel   ☐ ☐ pike
☐ ☐ pilchard   ☐ ☐ John Dory
☐ ☐ flounder   ☑ ☑ sprat   RO
☐ ☐ megrim   ☐ ☐ red mullet RW
☑ ☑ bream   ☐ ☐ sea bream   RW
☐ ☐ bass   ☑ ☐ whitebait   RO

9 Gutted, flattened, salted, cold-smoked herring are called:

☐ bloaters
☑ kippers
☑ buckling
☐ smokies

10 What is a *red herring*?

herrings which have been salted + then smoked.

11 Describe the service of three smoked fish.

1 Haddock fumé poché.

2 kippers - breakfast grilled.

3 Smoked salmon. Thinly sliced.

12 Is fish smoked at a temperature of 33 °C or 43 °C?

13 Hot-smoked fish is cured at a temperature of:
- [ ] 65–70 °C
- [ ] 70–80 °C
- [ ] 80–85 °C
- [ ] 85–90 °C

14 Explain the difference between the *London* and the *Scottish cure*, used when smoking salmon.

15 What is a *buckling*?

Whole smoked herring.

16 Name three fish which are canned.

1 tuna. 2 sardines. 3 salmon.

17 Kippers are produced from:
- [ ] codling
- [x] herring
- [ ] whiting
- [ ] haddock

18 Name three fish which may be smoked.

1 haddock 2 salmon 3 herring.

19 Caviar is obtained from:
- [ ] salmon
- [ ] skate
- [x] sturgeon
- [ ] hake

20 The conger eel is larger than the eel: true/false. F.

21 Mackerel must be used fresh because the flesh deteriorates very quickly.

22 Name three British rivers in which salmon are fished.

1 _Severn._   2 _Tay._   3 _Dee_

23 Rollmops are
☐ pickled rolled sprat fillets
☑ pickled rolled herring fillets
☐ pickled rolled haddock fillets
☐ smoked rolled haddock fillets

24 Name three fish which may be eaten smoked and which are not cooked apart from this smoking process.

1 _kippers_   2   3

25 What have the following in common?

anchovies   eels   herring   salmon   sprats   tunny fish
all oily fish.

26 Which fish is served jellied? _eels_ .

27 A salmon weighing less than 3½ kg is known as a _Grilse_ .

28 The sea-fish similar in appearance to salmon is:
☐ tunny   ☐ rainbow trout
☐ trout   ☑ salmon trout

29 Sardines are only used when tinned: true/false.
_F_

30 Are trout fished from rivers, lakes or the sea?
Rivers + lakes.

31 Which fish is used for serving _au bleu_?
trout.

32 What is tunny?
☐ baby turbot   ☑ a very large fish
☐ a quantity of trout   ☐ a kind of fishing boat

33 Which is the turbot and which is the brill?

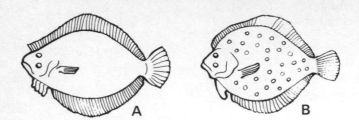

A   B

34 Whitebait are the fry of young _____.

35 Whitebait can be cooked in a variety of ways: true/false.

F.

36 Name the fish which has 'wings'. *Skate.*

37 Halibut is a white flat fish which can weigh up to:

☐ 50 kg   ☐ 75 kg   ☐ 100 kg   ☐ 150 kg

38 Which is considered to be the best of the flat fish?

☐ plaice   ☑ Dover sole ☐ lemon sole ☐ witch

39 What is the current market price of Dover sole?

40 The average weight of a turbot is:

☐ ½–1 kg   ☐ 1½–2 kg
☐ 2½–3 kg   ☐ 3½–4 kg

41 Name three popular round sea-fish.

1 *Cod.*   2 *haddock*   3

42 Explain what is meant by *en goujons*?

fish e.g plaice, sole, cut into thin strips to represent the fish goudgeons

43 How can you distinguish a whole cod from a whole haddock?

thumb mark on side & is lighter in colour

44 Which of the following is easy to digest and therefore suitable for invalid cookery?

☐ red mullet   ☐ herring

☐ salmon   ☑ whiting

45 Which is the more expensive: witch, lemon or Dover sole?

Dover.

46 The texture of monkfish is:

☐ flaky loose   ☐ firm close

☐ soft smooth   ☐ flaky firm

47 What has eight arms, is 6–12 ins long and has a mottled skin?

48 Give three methods of cooking the answer to Q47:

1   2   3

44 In what category are the following:

crawfish   cockles   cuttlefish   crayfish

Mollascans

50 Name the three types of scallops.

1   2   3

51 What is the purchasing unit of oysters?

☐ singles   ☐ ½ dozen

☐ tens   ☑ dozens

52 Shellfish is easily digested: true/false. *F*

53 Why is a little vinegar used in the cooking of shellfish?

to make fish fibres more digestable.

54 Why, if possible, is it best to buy shellfish alive?

to ensure freshness -

55 Arrange the following in order of size – smallest first.

☐ shrimps   ☐ lobster   ☐ prawn   ☐ crawfish

1   *3*   *2*   *4*

56 The colour of live lobster is:

☐ red ☐ orange ☐ green ☑ bluish-black

57 Hen lobsters are distinguished from cock lobsters by broader/
narrower tail: true/false. *f*

58 From which lobster can we obtain coral? hen/cock.

Hen

59 Identify the following

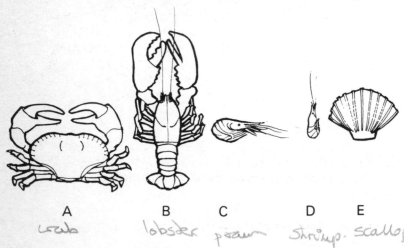

A   B   C   D   E

Crab   *lobster*   *prawn*   *Shrimp.* *Scallop*

60 The name given to shell fish soup is:

☐ soupe ☐ purée ☐ velouté
☑ bisque

61   Which is a crawfish and which a crayfish?

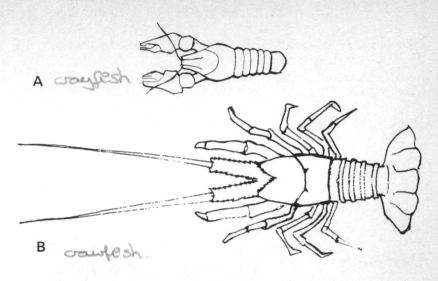

A   crayfish

B   crawfesh.

62   There is usually more flesh on a hen crab, but the flesh is
     considered to be of inferior quality to that of the cock crab:
     true/false.   True

63   By what two features of the crab tail can you distinguish a hen
     crab from a cock crab?

     1   Han tael broader

     2   "   " pinkey en colour, cocke teil whiler.

64   Which is the odd one out and why?

     ☐ Whitstable ☐ Chelmsford ☐ Colchester ☐ Helford

65   The majority of oysters eaten in Britain are consumed raw:
     true/false.   T

66   When are English oysters in season?   Sept →April.

67   Name two countries from which we import oysters during the
     summer months.

     1 Holland   2 Portugal.

                France.

68 Name two essential purchasing points of quality for mussels.

1 *tightly closed*   2 *shell fresh*

69 Mussels may be served hot or cold: true/false.

True

70 Why are scallops so dirty when fished out of the sea?

found on seabed

71 Why do we retain the deep shell of the scallop?

to service + there game + decoration

72 Name two fish roes that are popular eaten on their own.

1 *caviar*   2 *taramasalata*

6 Vegetables

pages 122–130

1 What is the nutritional value of root vegetables?

2 List ten vegetables available all the year round.

1 *carrots*	2	3	4
5	6	7	8
9	10		

3 Little protein or carbohydrate is found in green vegetables: true/false. *T.*

4 Fresh green vegetables are rich in ___*calcium*___ and ___*iron*___.

5 Describe good quality cabbage in four or five words.

bright in colour, crisp + tightly closed leaves

6 Fresh green vegetables should be stored in:

☐ the containers they are delivered in
☑ on well ventilated racks
☐ vegetable bins
☐ the refrigerator

7 Fresh vegetables and fruit are living _organisms_ and will lose _quality_ quickly if not properly _stored_ and handled.

8 Because of air cargo transport, many fruits and vegetables are in season the whole year round: true/false. T

9 Name two types of artichoke.

1 Jerusalem   2 globe

10 Name three types of fresh bean.

1 Runner beans 2 Mangetout 3 French.

11 What are the two chief types of mushroom?

1   2

12 What are two alternative names for sweetcorn?

13 Name three types of vegetables that can be purchased in dehydrated form.

1 Mushrooms   2 onions _   3 pot.
 carrots

14 Tick the methods by which vegetables are preserved.

☑ canning   ☑ pickling   ☑ freezing   ☑ dehydrating
☑ drying   ☐ smoking   ☑ salting

15 Name three vegetables available in dried form.

1 mushrooms . 2 peas   3 beans .

16 Name three popular pickled vegetables.

1 onions.   2 beetroot   3 gherkins

17 Name six vegetables available in deep-frozen form.

1 *cauli.* 2 *sweetcorn.* 3 *peas*

4 *carrots* 5 *brocolli* 6 *broadbeans*

18 What is the difference between *cos* and a *cabbage lettuce*?

soft, with frilly coloured edge, compact

19 Which group is obtainable fresh in winter?

☑ sprouts, celery, swedes, parsnips
☐ marrow, sprouts, asparagus, cabbage
☐ runner beans, carrots, swedes, sweetcorn
☐ peas, parsnips, aubergine, seakale

20 What is another name for salsify?

21 A long narrow root plant used in soups, salads and as a vegetable
is called s_____.

22 Mooli is:

☑ long, white and thick
☐ long, red and thick
☐ short, white and thin
☐ short, red and thin

23 How may sweet potatoes and yams be used?

24 Describe the difference between sweet potatoes and yams.

25 For what purpose are corn salad, radiccio and cress used?

26 Describe radiccio.

27 The pea eaten in its entirety is known by three names:

1   2   3

28 Give four uses of avocado.

1 *Avocat vinaigrette.*   2

3   4

29 What are squash, pumpkin, courgette and aubergine classified as?

fruits

30 What vegetable is described as resembling a fat pine cone with overlapping green edible leaves connected to an edible base?

artichoke.

31 Name and describe four types of fungi.

1

2

3

4

7 Fruit

pages 130–135

1 Give two examples of each fruit classification:

Soft fruit	1 *rasp.*	2 *strawberry.*
Hard fruit	1 *apple*	2 *pear*
Stone fruit	1 *apricot.*	2 *plum.*
Citrus fruit	1 *lemon*	2 *lime*
Tropical	1 *melon*	2 *banana.*

2 Name four English soft fruits in addition to the two in the previous question.

1 *blackberries.*   2 *blackcurrants*

3 *loganberries.*   4 *redcurrants*

3 Which are the three most used citrus fruits?

1 orange   2 lemon   3 grapefruit

4 Are the fruits given in your previous answer available all the year round? yes/no. *y*

5 Rhubarb is in season during:

☐ Autumn   ☐ Winter
☑ Spring   ☐ Summer

6 From which month do English soft fruits come into season?

☐ April   ☐ June
☑ July   ☐ August

7 Place the following in order of availability during the year:

☐ gooseberries ☐ cherries   ☐ damsons   ☐ currants
☐ raspberries   ☐ plums

8 Imported apples and pears are available all the year round: true/false.

9 Which of the following fruit are available in dried form?

☐ apples   ☐ gooseberries ☑ apricots   ☑ damsons
☐ strawberries ☐ pears   ☐ rhubarb   ☑ figs

10 Plums when dried are called:

11 Small grapes when dried are called:

currants

12 Medium-sized grapes when dried are called:

raisins

13 Large grapes when dried are called:

sultanas

14 Solid packed apples are apples which have been peeled, cored, quatered and:

☐ packed tightly in cases
☐ frozen and packed in water in tins
☑ packed in water in tins
☐ packed in large barrels

44

15 What are candied, glacé and crystallised fruits?

fruits dipped in syrup, dried + then dipped again.

16 Citrus fruits are a source of vitamin __C__.

17 Bananas should be stored in a refrigerator: true/false.

F

18 Give an example of a different fruit bought in each of the following.

1 a tray *avocado.*   2 a case *apples.*

3 a punnet *strawberries* 4 a box *Melon*

19 Give an example of a:

1 candied fruit *– orange + lemon peel.*

2 crystallised fruit *–*

3 glacé fruit *– cherries*

20 From which country do we import most of our glacé, crystallised and candied fruit?

☐ Italy   ☐ Holland
☐ Spain   ☑ France

21 What kinds of fruit are the following?

1 Blenheim Orange *apples.*   2 William *– pear*

3 Bramley's seedling *– apple* 4 Avocado *a green skinned pear.*

5 Comice *pear.*   6 Cantaloup *– Melon*

22 Give the name of a chicken dish which includes banana as part of the garnish.

Maryland chicken

23 Name a fish dish garnished with banana.

filet de sole caprice.

24 Name three fruits which have both dessert and cooking varieties.

1 *bannana.* 2 *pear*   3 *apple*

45

25 Marmalade can be made from:

1 _orange_   2 _lemons_   3

26 Bananas can be grilled, fried or eaten raw: true/false.

_T._

27 Which fruit is used to garnish fish Véronique?

28 Name three types of melon.

1 _Honeydew_ 2 _Cantaloup_ 3 _water_

29 Is a honeydew melon round or oval?

oval.

30 Name four tropical fruits; briefly describe them and give an example of their use.

Fruit	Description	Use
1 _banana._		_banana fritters_
2 _pineapple_		_grilled gammon pineapple._
3 _Melon._		_melon frappé._
4 _papaya._		_fruit salad._

31 Which fruit berry sauce is served with roast turkey?

☐ blackberry
☑ cranberry
☐ gooseberry
☐ mulberry

32 Name two varieties of each fruit below.

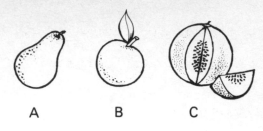

A   B   C

A   Conference, William.

B   Cox's. Golden Delicious.

C

8   Nuts

pages 135–136

1 Nuts are a source of:

2 When purchasing nuts, select those which are heavy for their size: true/false.

3 Name three popular dessert nuts.

     1   2   3

4 Which nut has probably the most uses in pastry and confectionery work?

     ☐ almond   ☐ Brazil
     ☐ walnut   ☐ pecan

5 Give four examples of the use of nuts in pastry work.

     1

     2

     3

     4

6 Which nut is used in desiccated form for certain curry dishes?

7 Small green nuts used for decorating are called:
- ☐ filberts
- ☐ cobs
- ☐ adagio
- ☑ pistachio

8 Name three types of nuts that are served salted.

1 cashew.　　2　　　　3

9 Match the correct names to these nuts.

Chestnut	Walnut	Coconut	Almond	Brazil
1	2	3	4	5

9 Eggs

pages 136–140

1 When assessing quality points for buying eggs, the eggshell should be c____n, well s____d, s____g and slightly r____h.

2 When an egg is broken, if it is fresh, there ought to be a high p____n of thick w____e to thin w____e.

3 The yolk should be f____m, r____d and of good e____n c____r.

4 What happens to the white of egg if it is kept too long?

thick white → then white + water passes into the yolk.

5   What happens to the yolk of egg if the egg is kept too long?

loses strength + begins to flatten

6   Eggs should be stored in a:
☐ cold, very dry place   ☐ cool, dry place
☐ cold, damp place   ☑ cool but not too dry place

7   The ideal storage place for eggs is in a refrigerator without any strong smelling foods at a temperature of:
☑ 0°–5°   ☐ 18°–20°
☐ 10°–15°   ☐ 22°–25°

8   Why should strong smelling foods not be stored near eggs?

shells are porous ∴ would absorb smells.

9   Give three examples of strong smelling foods which should not be stored near eggs.

1 *onions*   2 *garlic*   3 *fish, cheese*

10 If there were a shortage of hens' eggs, which other two birds' eggs could be used in place?

1 t*urkey*   2 g*oose*   f*owl*

11 State the nutritional value of eggs.

high in protein

12 Give examples of the uses of eggs.
eg   thickening   -   baked egg custard, mayonnaise
       clarifying   -   *consommé*
       binding   -   *duchess pots, vienna steaks*
       coating   -   *egg wash pastry, croquette pots.*
       colouring   -   *egg custard.*

13 Name the bacteria which have affected some eggs causing food poisoning.

salmonella

14 Which two groups of people are most likely to be affected by the bacteria given in your answer to Q13?

1 *the elderly.*   2 *young children.*

10 Milk

pages 140–144

1 Why is milk regarded as the almost perfect food?

2 Unlike eggs, milk will not absorb strong smells from other foods if kept uncovered in a refrigerator: true/false.

3 Milk is pasteurised in order to:

☐ improve its keeping quality
☐ improve its flavour
☐ concentrate the strength
☐ kill harmful bacteria

4 Pasteurised milk is heated for:

☐ 15 seconds at 72 °C
☐ 20 seconds at 52 °C
☐ 25 seconds at 62 °C
☐ 30 seconds at 72 °C

5 What is UHT milk?

6 Under sterile conditions UHT milk will keep for:

☐ 4 days   ☐ 4 weeks
☐ 4 months   ☐ 14 months

7 Homogenised milk has been:

☐ pasteurised twice
☐ drawn from a herd of pedigree cows
☐ treated so that the cream is dispersed throughout the milk
☐ pasteurised and UHT treated

8   Sterilised milk is produced from milk which has been:
    ☐ homogenised   ☐ condensed
    ☐ pasteurised   ☐ evaporated

9   What is the ingredient in cream that causes it to be
    able to be whipped? B_____.

10 What is the essential difference between single and double cream?

11 Devonshire and clotted cream are two different names for the
    same type of cream: true/false.

12 With what would clotted cream be served?

13 If cream is overwhipped it turns to:
    ☐ yoghurt   ☐ cheese
    ☐ margarine   ☐ butter

14 Is there any remedy for over-whipped fresh cream? yes/no.

15 When whipping fresh cream the cream must be:
    ☐ warm   ☐ cold
    ☐ at blood heat   ☐ almost frozen

16 Yoghurt is prepared from milk: true/false.

11   Fats and oils

pages 144–147

1   Fats should be kept in a cold store or refrigerator: true/false.

2   Why should butter be kept away from strong smelling foods?

3   It takes approximately _____ litre of cream to produce
    _____ kg of butter.

4 Butter is an e_____y food because it has a very high
f_____ content.

5 If kept too long butter becomes:

☐ saturated   ☐ liquid
☐ rancid   ☐ pasteurised

6 Why is salt added to some makes of butter in its production?

7 Butter is imported in large amounts from all but one of the
following countries. Indicate the odd one out:

☐ New Zealand   ☐ France   ☐ Denmark
☐ Australia   ☐ Austria   ☐ Holland

8 Butter when used for shallow frying is:

☐ homogenised   ☐ condensed
☐ sterilised   ☐ clarified

9 Margarine is nutritionally inferior to butter: true/false.

10 Margarine is manufactured from milk and a
v_____ oil.

11 Margarine can be used in place of butter for all culinary purposes:
true/false.

12 Name three types of oil used to produce margarine.

1   2   3

13 Lard is the rendered fat from:

☐ ox   ☐ pig
☐ sheep   ☐ goat

14 The fat content of lard is almost:

☐ 100%   ☐ 90%   ☐ 80%   ☐ 70%

15 Suet is obtained from the:

☐ kidney region of baconer pig
☐ liver region of pork
☐ heart region of veal
☐ kidney region of beef

16 Clarified animal fat is called _____.

17 Oils are fats which are liquid at room temperature: true/false.

18 Name three varieties of vegetable oil.

1   2   3

19 Will a good vegetable oil keep indefinitely at room temperature: yes/no?

20 Which of the vegetable oils is considered to have the most flavour?

☐ olive   ☐ groundnut   ☐ maize

21 Name three countries from which olive oil is imported.

1   2   3

22 The best oils are almost free from:

1   2   3

23 What is an essential requirement for an oil that is to be used for deep-frying?

24 Which of the following would you use for deep-frying?

☐ vegetable oil   ☐ dripping
☐ maize oil   ☐ olive oil

25 Give the reason for your answer to the previous question.

26 Why should oils be free from moisture?

12 Cheese

pages 147–150

1 Cheese is made from _cows / ewes / goat milk_

2 List the four main types of cheese and give an example of each.

   1 _Hard_

   2 _Semi-hard_

   3 _soft / cream_

   4 _blue vein_

3 Which cheese is made from goat's milk?
   - ☑ Parmesan
   - ☐ Chèvre
   - ☐ Edam
   - ☐ Brie

4 Which cheese is made from ewe's milk?
   - ☐ Gorgonzola
   - ☐ Stilton
   - ☑ Roquefort
   - ☐ Danish blue

5 Where should cheese be stored?
   cool, dry + well ventilated

6 Why is cheese a nutritious food?
   fat, protein, mineral salts + vit A+D all present

7 The skin or rind of cheese should not show spots of
   m _ould_ as this is a sign of damp storage.

8 When cut, cheese should not give off an over-strong
   s _mell_ or any indication of a _ammonia_.

9 Name three hard, three soft and three blue vein cheeses.

   1 _Cheddar_   2 _Camembert_   3 _Stilton_

   1 _Leister_   2 _brie_   3 _Danish blue_

   1 _Cheshire_   2 _Pommel del sel_   3 _Lymeswold_

54

10   Hard, semi-hard and blue vein cheese when cut should not
     appear __dry__ .

11   Soft cheese when cut should not appear r~unny~ but should
     have a delicate c~reamy~ consistency.

12   The chief fermenting agent used in cheese making is:
     ☐ junket   ☐ plunket
     ☑ rennet   ☐ sonnet

13   Name four English varieties of cheese.
     1   2

     3   4

14   Delete the odd one out in each line:
     1 Cheddar, Cheshire, Camembert, Gruyère, Parmesan
     2 Brie, Carré de L'Est, Demi Swiss, Gorgonzola
     3 Stilton, Bel Paese, Roquefort, Danish Blue
     4 Caerphilly, St Paulin, Emmental, Pont L'Eveque

15   Name one cheese from each of the following countries:
     France   brie
     Italy   Gorgonzola .
     Holland   Edam .
     Switzerland   Gruyere .
     Denmark   Danish blue .
     England   Cheddar

16   The hardest cheese which is produced for grating is:
     ☐ Port Salut   ☑ Parmesan
     ☐ Pommel demi-Swiss   ☐ Bel Paese

17   The famous rich double cream cheese with blue veins made in
     England is
     ☑ Stilton   ☐ Double Gloucester
     ☐ Caerphilly   ☐ Dorset Blue vinny

55

18 Two of the most popular French cheeses are

☑ Camembert
☐ St Paulin
☐ Carré de l'Est
☑ Brie

19 Identify these cheeses.

1 Edam.   2   3 brie   4 Gruyere

20 Rearrange the following cheeses to fit the correct descriptions:

☑ white, soft, crumbly; clean, 1 Double Gloucester
   mild flavour
☐ orange-red, buttery open   2 Cheddar
   texture; delicate creamy
   flavour
☑ white with blue veins, soft, 3 Lancashire
   close texture; strong flavour
☑ golden colour, close texture; 4 Stilton
   clean, mellow, nutty flavour

21 Rearrange the following cheeses to fit the countries of origin:

☐ Caboc   1 Greece
☑ Roquefort   2 Switzerland
☐ Ricotta   3 Holland
☐ Cambazola   4 Italy
☑ Edam   5 Germany
☑ Gruyère   6 France
☑ Fetta   7 Scotland

22 What do the following cheeses have in common?

Gorgonzola   Roquefort   Cambazola   Stilton

23 What do the following cheeses have in common?

Quark   Fromage frais   Curd cheese   Cottage cheese

56

24 Natural yoghurt should contain no colour, p_____,
stabilisers or t_____ and may be fortified with vitamins
____ and ____.

25 Natural yoghurt may be flavoured with:
1   2   3

26 Smetana is a low fat product, a cross between soured cream and
yoghurt: true/false.

27 Describe and explain the use of:
1 fromage frais

2 quark

3 natural yoghurt

4 smetana

13 Cereals

pages 150–154

1 All the following cereals are used in catering: true/false.
wheat, oats, barley, maize, rice, tapioca, sago, arrowroot

2 All cereals contain large amounts of __starch__.

3 Flour is produced from __wheat__.

4 Whole grain cereals provide vitamin:
☐ A
☑ B
☐ D

5 In what atmosphere should flour be stored?
Dry & well ventilated.

6 What is the difference between strong and soft flour?

The gluten content - strong has more

7 Name three foods for which soft flour is suitable.

1 *biscuits.*   2 *thickening soups + sauces.*   3 *butters*

8 Name three foods for which strong flour is suitable.

1 *bread*   2 *puff pastry*   3 *Italian pastas.*

9 What percentage of the whole grain is contained in:

1 wholemeal flour   *100 %*

2 wheatmeal flour   *90 %*

3 white flour?   *70 - 72 %*

10 What is added to white flour to make it self raising?

cream of tartar + bicarb. of soda

11 What is semolina?

granulated hard flour from the central part of wheat grain

12 Which is the odd one out and why?

☐ vermicelli   ☐ spaghetti   ☐ macaroni   ☐ minestroni

13 Oats have the highest food value of all the cereals: true/false.

True

14 The chief use of oats is:

☐ gruel   ☐ oat cakes
☑ porridge   ☐ Scotch broth

15 From which cereal is cornflour obtained?

☐ wheat   ☐ oats
☑ maize   ☐ barley

16 Maize, sweetcorn, corn, corn on the cob are different names for the same food: true/false. *true.*

17 When cooked long grain rice has a ___*firm*___ structure.

18 When cooked short grain rice has a _soft_ _____ structure.

19 What is obtained from:

1 the roots of the cassava plant? *Tapioca*

2 the pith of a certain palm? *Sago*

3 the roots of the West Indian Maranta Plant? *arrowroot*

20 Why is arrowroot particularly suitable for thickening clear sauces?
Transparent when boiled

21 Arrowroot is suitable for invalids because it is easily digested:
true/false. *True.*

14 Raising agents

pages 155–157

1 Name three food processes in which air is used as a raising agent.
1 *sifting flour.* 2   3

2 Baking powder is a chemical raising agent: true/false.
True

3 List five hints on using baking powder.
1 *Mix powder thoroughly into flour.*

2 *Measure accurately.*

3 *Store probably - tight fitting lid.*

4 *Too much - cake collapse in middle*

5 *Insufficient close, heavy texture.*

4 What is yeast?

☑ a form of plant life
☐ a chemically produced raising agent
☐ concentrated hops
☐ double strength baking powder

5 State four essential storage and quality points for fresh yeast.

1 *Fresh + Moist*

2 *Pleasant smell*

3 *crumble easily*

4 *Pale grey in colour*

6 Yeast should always be used at room temperature: true/false.
   True

7 Yeast contains Vitamin B: true/false.
   True + rich in protein

8 To enable yeast to grow which conditions are necessary?

☐ moisture, heat, salt
☐ cold liquid, sugar, proving
☐ hot liquid, salt, sugar
☑ blood heat liquid, sugar, proving

9 Does salt retard the working of yeast? yes/no.
   Yes

10 Above which temperature is yeast destroyed?

☐ 12 °C   ☐ 22 °C
☐ 42 °C   *over* ☑ 52 °C

11 Yeast can withstand low temperature without damage: true/false.
   True

12 Why should yeast dough be well kneaded?
   to make an elastic dough + to distribute the yeast evenly

13 Give another word meaning *kneading*.
   working

14 *Proving* a yeast dough means

☐ letting it rest
☐ cutting it back
☑ allowing it to double in size
☐ it has satisfied the customers

15 Name six items that are made using yeast.

1 bread doughs .   2 frying batters

3 bun doughs eg   4 croissants .
doughnuts ?

5 Danish pastry .   6 babas, savarins

16 What causes over-proving?

too much heat / uneven heat , too much time .

15 Sugar

page 157

1 Sugar is invaluable for producing energy: ~~true~~/false. True

2 Sugar is obtained from sugar beet _____ and sugar cane _____.

3 What percentage of pure sugar is contained in sugar?

☑ 100%   ☐ 60%
☐ 80%   ☐ 40%

4 Demerara sugar is

☑ brown sugar   ☐ lump sugar
☐ coffee sugar   ☐ fine caster sugar

5 Brown sugar is unrefined: true/false. True .

6 List the following in order of fineness with the finest first:

icing sugar, granulated sugar, caster sugar

1 icing .

2 caster

3 granulated

7 What is loaf sugar?

cube sugar - sugar crystals compressed

8   Give an example of the use of each of these:

    1 glucose   *confectionery*.

    2 syrup

    3 treacle

16   Cocoa and chocolate

page 158

1   Cocoa is a powder produced from the beans of the cacao tree: true/false.   *True*.

2   Does cocoa have any food value?

    Yes — protein, starch, iron.

3   Chocolate is produced from cocoa mass, fine sugar and cocoa butter: true/false.   *True*.

4   Give three uses of chocolate couverture.

    1 *icings*   2 *sauces*   3 *butter creams*.

17   Coffee

pages 159–160

1   Name four varieties of coffee.

    1 *Kenya*.   2 *Mocha*

    3 *Java*.   4 *Brazil*

2   What is the correct way to store coffee?

    airtight containers, well ventilated.

3   Coffee has some food value: true/false.

    False.

4 Name the methods of coffee making which apply to the illustrated equipment.

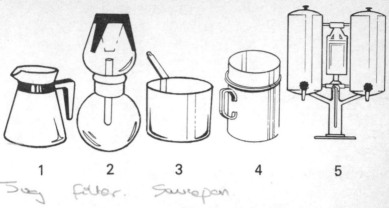

1	2	3	4	5

Jug   filter.   Saucepan.

5 List six points to follow when making coffee.

1 Good quality, freshly ground.

2 Freshly drawn + freshly boiled.

3 If milk, use hot milk.

4 Coffee should be strained off toward bitter taste

5 Scrupulously clean equipment.

6 Measure coffee accurately.

6 How much coffee is required to produce 1 litre?

300 - 360 gms.

18 Tea

pages 160–161

1 Name five tea producing countries.

1 India.   2 Darjeeling. 3 China

4 Assam   5 Java.

2 Tea without sugar and/or milk has no nutritional value: true/false.

True

3 Why must tea be kept in airtight containers?

to prevent it absorbing moisture + odours.

4 What are the five golden rules for making good tea?

1 *Use a good tea.*

2 *freshly drawn + boiled water.*

3 *Heat the pot - infusion of tea*

4 *Use boiling water.*

5 *Allow tea to brew sufficiently.*

19 Pulses

pages 161–162

1 Pulses are dried s_*seeds*_ of plants which form
p_*ods*_.

2 Name three types of pulse.
1 *butter beans* 2 *lentils.* 3 *green split peas.*

3 Pulses are a good source of protein: true/false.
True

4 How would you describe the following:

1 flageolets

2 haricot

3 dahl

5 Which pulse items fit the following descriptions?
1 pink splotched mottled colour

2 resembles the kernel of a small hazel nut

3 small, brown, knobbly

6 What could these beans be used for?

1 mung beans

2 soya beans

3 red kidney beans

20 Herbs

pages 162–164

1 What value have herbs from the nutritional point of view?

☐ To provide body regulating processes
☐ Enables starch to be converted to sugar
☐ Creates energy from carbohydrate
☑ Stimulates the flow of gastric juices

2 Name five common herbs and state a suitable use for each.

1 bayleaves = sauces + soups bouquet garni.

2 basil - tomato sauce.

3 mint - new potatoes.

4 rosemary - stuffings, stews roasts eg lamb

5 oregana - Italian + greek style cooking
e.g pasta.

3 Herbs may be used f̲r̲e̲s̲h̲_____ but the majority are
d̲r̲i̲e̲d̲._____.

4 What is it in the leaves of herbs that gives the characteristic smell and flavour?

☐ pollen   ☐ flower buds
☑ oil   ☐ the stems

5 Which herb is a member of the onion family and has a delicate onion flavour?
Chives.

6 Which is the strong pungent herb that aids the stomach to digest rich fatty meat such as pork, duck, goose?

Sage

7 What is the composition of fines-herbes?

chervil, tarragon, parsley.

8 Angelica is a crystallised

☐ leaf ☐ seed ☐ root ☑ stem

21 Spices

pages 164–167

1 Spices are a variety of fruits, seeds, roots, flowers or bark of different trees or shrubs: true/false. *T*

2 Allspice is another name for mixed spice: true/false.

3 Cloves are:

☑ unopened seed pods of a tree from Zanzibar
☐ the fruit of a shrub from Penang
☐ the flower buds of a shrub from Morocco
☐ unopened flower buds of a tree from Madagascar

4 Which spice is associated with the cooking of apples?

cinnamon

5 Which spice is the bark of the small branches of the c _cinnamon_ shrub?

6 Which tropical tree bears a fruit like an apricot which when ripe has a kernel which is _nutmeg_ . The kernel is covered with a bright red covering which is _mace_ .

7 Name four spices which go into mixed spice.

1 *allspice* 2 *cinnamon*

3 *cloves* 4 *coriander*

ginger nutmeg

66

8   State a different use for each of these:

1 nutmeg   – *rice pudding – milk puddings.*

2 saffron   –   *colouring rice.*

3 cinnamon   –   *baked apples, apple pies.*

4 carraway   –   *seed cake + breads*

9   Saffron is the dried stigmas from a crocus grown chiefly in:
☑ Spain   ☐ Portugal   ☐ Italy

10   Which of these items are used with fish dishes:
☐ dill seeds   ☐ anise   ☐ fennel seeds

11   What are the following and what are their uses:
1 fenugreek

2 garam masala

3 cardamon

4 Chinese five spice powder

22   Condiments

pages 167–169

1   What causes the difference between white and black peppercorns?
white peppers corns is bpc with outer skin removed.

2   Why is salt necessary in the diet?
stabilising bodily fluids + preventing muscular cramp.

3   What happens to salt if it is not kept dry?
it absorbs moisture.

4   From what is pepper obtained?
berry of a tropical shrub.

67

5   Which is the hotter – cayenne or paprika?

6   Paprika is a:
    ☐ type of herb   ☑ mild pepper
    ☐ oriental spice   ☐ kind of mustard

7   Paprika is used in a specific dish known as ___Goulash___. *Hungarian*

8   From which country did the dish named in the previous question originate? *Hungary*

9   In which part of Great Britain is mustard grown?
    ☑ East Anglia   ☐ East Lanarkshire
    ☐ Scilly Isles   ☐ Lancashire

10 Malt vinegar is made from oats: true/false. *True – barley*

11 Name three types of vinegar.
    1 *Malt*   2 *white/red wine*   3 *spirit*

12 Name the most expensive vinegar which has the most delicate flavour. *Red/white wine*

13 State two uses of vinegar other than preservation.
    1 *condiment – on its own or salad dressings.*   2 *as a marinade*

23   Colourings, flavourings and essences

pages 169–170

1   What colour is cochineal? *red*

2   Match the colours to their culinary sources.
    ☐ green   1 tumeric
    ☐ red   2 chlorophyl
    ☐ brown   3 cochineal
    ☐ yellow   4 blackjack

3   What could anchovy essence be used for? *fish cakes + sauces*

68

24 Grocery, delicatessen and confectionery goods

pages 170–175

1   What is *aspic jelly*?

a clear, savoury jelly used in larder work & coating (cold) fried chaud dishes.

2   *Bombay duck* is:

☐ a small Indian duck
☐ an eastern type of sweet
☑ dried fillet of fish
☐ a Chinese hors-d'oeuvre

3   Caviar is obtained from:

☐ cod   ☐ salmon
☐ carp   ☑ sturgeon

4   The finest caviar comes from

☐ France, Italy, or Spain
☑ Russia, Persia, or Romania
☐ Hungary, Yugoslavia, or Arabia
☐ Holland, Belgium, or Denmark

5   *Cèpes* are a:

☑ species of French mushroom   ☐ kind of Italian pasta
☐ type of French pancake   ☐ variety of Italian pear

6   What is *foie gras*?

livers of specially fattened geese.

7   *Galantine* is a:

☑ cooked meat preparation   ☐ kind of haggis
☐ type of salami   ☐ special vegetable dish

8   Name the two forms in which gelatine is available and give an example of its use.

1   2

9   What are *gherkins*?

a pickled variety of cucumbers.

10 Name the three main varieties of olive.

1 M*anzanilla*

2 S*panish*

3 B*lack*   Q*ueens*

11 With which countries are the following associated?

1 frog's legs   *France*   2 sauerkraut

3 haggis   *Scotland*   4 poppadum

5 Parma ham   *Italy*   6 Stilton

7 foie gras   *Strasbourg*   8 truffles

9 olives   10 escargots

12 Give an example of the use of:

1 capers   *Tartar sauce. cape sauce*

2 gherkins

3 olives   *garnishing eg escalope de veau viennoise.*

13 Walnuts are pickled after/<u>before</u> the shell has hardened.

14 *Poppadums* are:

☐ poppy seeds   ☐ an exotic oriental fruit
☐ Indian breakfast cereal   ☑ thin round biscuits

15 Potted shrimps are preserved in:

☐ margarine   ☐ vegetable oil
☐ oil   ☑ butter

16 *Rollmops* are:

☐ curled anchovies
☐ dainty bread rolls
☑ rolled herring fillets
☐ rolled kipper fillets

17 Sauerkraut is made from:

☑ white cabbage   □ red cabbage
□ green cabbage   □ a mixture of all three

18 The ideal weight of a salmon for smoking is:

□ 2½–5 kilos   ☑ 6–7½ kilos
□ 10–11½ kilos   □ 12½–15 kilos

19 At which course would smoked salmon be served?

1st course, hors' d'oeuves, canapes.

20 What are *escargots*?

snails.

21 How would escargots be served?

as a 1st course, in special dish

22 *Truffles* are a f__oogie__ and the most famous area in which
they are found is the P__erigord__ region of France.

23 A *marron glacé* is a peeled and cooked chestnut preserved in syrup:
true/false. *t.*

24 *Honey* is a natural sugar produced by bees working upon the
n__ectar__ of f__lowers__.

25 *Pastillage* is a mixture of icing sugar and

☑ gum tragacanth   □ gum organic
□ gum grysanth   □ gum agnostic

26 Rennet is used for making:

□ aspic   ☑ junket
□ jelly   □ fondant

6

Purchasing, costing, control and storekeeping

pages 181–206

1 For purchasing commodities a s_____ k_____ of all commodities is essential.

2 Which guide to purchasing should be followed?

☐ the cheapest is the best
☐ compare quality with price
☐ the dearest is always the best
☐ the best quality is the cheapest

3 List ten points which assist in the efficient buying of food.

1	2
3	4
5	6
7	8
9	10

4 Out-of-date price lists should be consulted: true/false.

5 What do you understand by *portion control*?

6 Why should portion control be linked closely with the buying of food?

7 Better quality food usually gives a better yield than inferior quality food: true/false.

8 The golden rule to use when considering portion control is

f_____ p_____ for a f_____ p_____.

9 Indicate which points should be considered regarding portion control:

☐ the type of customer or establishment
☐ the Safety at Work Act
☐ the quality of the food
☐ the qualifications of the kitchen staff
☐ the buying price of the food
☐ the gas and electricity services available

10 Name six items of equipment that assist portion control.

1   2   3

4   5   6

11 Approximately how many portions of soup would be obtained from a litre?

☐ 1–2   ☐ 3–4
☐ 4–6   ☐ 7–8

12 Approximately how many portions of haddock would be obtained from 1 kg of haddock fillet?

☐ 2   ☐ 4
☐ 6   ☐ 8

13 Approximately how many portions would be obtained from 1 litre of custard?

☐ 16–24   ☐ 25–30
☐ 32–36   ☐ 40–50

14 Sausages are obtainable 12, 16, or 20 to the kg: true/false.

15 Approximately how many portions would be obtained from 1 kg of unpeeled old potatoes?

☐ 2–3 ☐ 4–6
☐ 7–8 ☐ 9–10

16 How many sheep's kidneys would be a portion?

☐ 1 ☐ 2 ☐ 3 ☐ 4

17 Briefly describe the differences between the following markets:

1 primary

2 secondary

3 tertiary

18 What is a *standard purchasing specification*?

19 List three advantages of standard purchasing specifications:

1

2

3

20 Give three objectives of a standard recipe:

1

2

3

21 Outline three of the main difficulties of controlling food:

1

2

3

22 Suggest three factors that can affect a food control system:

1

2

3

23 Fill in the gaps in this control cycle of daily operation:

Purchasing

_____

Storing and

_____

Preparing

24 For sales and volume forecasting to be of practical value the forecast must predict:

1 the total number of _____

2 the choice of _____ _____

25 List six factors which will affect the profitability of an establishment:

1   2

3   4

5   6

26 What are the advantages of an efficient costing system?

27 One costing system will suit any type of catering establishment: true/false.

28 What are the three main elements that make up the total cost of an item or a meal?

1 f_____ or m_____ cost

2 l_____

3 o_____

29 Food and materials are known as _____ costs.

Labour costs and overheads are known as _____ costs.

30 List six examples of item 3 in question 28.

1   2

3   4

5   6

31 Gross profit or kitchen profit is the difference between the

c_____ of the food and the s_____

p_____ of the food.

32 Net profit is the difference between the s_____

p_____ of the food (s_____) and the total cost.

33 Sales minus food cost =

Sales minus total cost =

Food cost plus gross profit =

34 Profit is expressed as a percentage of the _____ price.

35 Finding the food costs helps control costs, prices and profits: true/false.

36 Will an efficient food cost system help prevent waste and stealing? yes/no.

37 Sales less food cost =

☐ gross profit   ☐ gross price
☐ net profit   ☐ net price

38 In the metric system what do these refer to?

SI

g

m

ml

39 The caterer who gives the customer value for money, together with the type of food the customer wants, is well on his way to being successful: true/false.

Storekeeping

pages 195–206

1 A clean orderly food store run efficiently is essential in any catering establishment: true/false.

2 State three reasons for running an efficient food store.

  1

  2

  3

3 Why is it desirable for a food store to face north?

4 Why is good ventilation and freedom from dampness essential in a food store?

5 State six points necessary for a well-planned store.

1	2
3	4
5	6

6 To maintain good standards of hygiene what is essential with regard to:

  1 walls

  2 ceilings

  3 floors

  4 shelves

7   All store containers should be easy to clean and have tightly fitting lids: true/false.

8   Cleaning materials, because they have a strong smell, should be kept:

☐ on the lowest shelves in the store
☐ on the highest shelves in the store
☐ at one end of the store
☐ in a separate store

9   Name the two groups into which foods are divided for storage purposes:

1   2

10 What is the correct procedure with cases of tinned food?

☐ leave in the cases until required
☐ open case at one end so that cans can easily be removed
☐ unpack the cases and stack on shelves
☐ unpack the tins, inspect them and then stack on shelves.

11 Why should dented tins be used as soon as possible?

12 Briefly describe the layout of an efficient vegetable store.

13 Name four qualities of a good storekeeper.

1   2

3   4

14 First in first out is a good rule for issuing stores: true/false.

15 What are *requisitions*?

16 Complete the heading on this incomplete bin card:

17 Complete the heading on this stores ledger sheet:

18 Every time goods are received or issued, the appropriate entries should be made on both the stores ledger sheet and the bin card: true/false.

19 Explain the reason for your answer to the previous question.

20 What is a *departmental requisition book*?

21 Complete the headings on this departmental requisition book:

			DEPARTMENTAL REQUISITION BOOK					267
. . . .			Class.					
	Quan.	Price per Unit	Issued if Different		Unit	Code	£	

22 An order book is filled in every time the storekeeper wishes to have goods delivered: true/false.

23 An order book has:

☐ one copy ☐ two copies
☐ three copies ☐ four copies

24 Should all entries in the order book be signed? yes/no.

25 If you answered yes to the previous question, who should sign the orders?

☐ manager
☐ chef
☐ storekeeper
☐ finance officer

26 What is the purpose of the stock sheet?

27 Stock should be taken at regular intervals of:

☐ one week or one month
☐ two weeks or two months
☐ three weeks or three months
☐ four weeks or four months

28 What is the purpose of stock-taking?

29 What is a *spot check*?

☐ an inspection of food to see if germs or spots are present
☐ a check of a few random items of stock
☐ a check on the cleanliness of bin cards
☐ a check on all bin card entries

30 Delivery notes are sent with goods supplied as a means of

c_____g that everything ordered has been

d_____d.

31 What is the relationship between the delivery note and the
duplicate order sheet?

32 Invoices are sent out to clients setting out the cost of the goods
supplied or services rendered: true/false.

33 *Bill* is another name for an _____.

34 An invoice should be sent out:

☐ on the day the goods are sent out
☐ one month after the goods are sent out
☐ two months after the goods are sent out
☐ six months after the goods are sent out

35 What do the *terms of settlement* on a bill mean?

36 A credit note is issued stating:

☐ how much is owed to the company
☐ allowances made for adjustments and returnables
☐ how much credit the company allows
☐ allowances for staff meals

37 Statements show:

☐ the state of the company at the half year
☐ details of the purchases of the quarter
☐ summaries of invoices and credit notes for the previous month
☐ amounts of goods returned during the month

38 Give two examples of the use of credit notes:

1   2

39 When a client makes payment he or she usually pays by cheque. Will he or she also send back the statement? yes/no.

40 Who completes the statement and where is it finally kept?

41 Cash discount is discount allowed in consideration of p_____ payment.

42 Trade discount is discount allowed by one _____ to another.

43 *Gross price* is the price of an article before/after discount has been deducted.

44 *Net price* is the price of an article before/after discount has been deducted.

45 *Debit* indicates the monies coming in: true/false.

46 Make entries for Monday (Out), Wednesday (In) and Thursday (Out) to agree final columns.

Daily Stores Issues Sheet

Com-modity	Unit	Stock in hand	Monday In	Monday Out	Tuesday In	Tuesday Out	Wednesday In	Wednesday Out	Thursday In	Thursday Out	Friday In	Friday Out	Total pur-chases	Total issues	Total stock
Butter	kg	27												5	22
Flour	Sacks	2											1	1	2
Olive oil	Litres	8												1½	6½
Spices	30 g packs	8												8	4	12
Peas, tin	A10	30												9	21

7

Kitchen equipment

pages 207–242

1 Why is the correct use, care and maintenance of kitchen
equipment so important?

2 Add two points to the following which are important for the
maintenance and care of kitchen equipment.

1 Periodic checks

2 Careful usage

3 Following maker's instructions

4 Reporting faults

5 Keeping a log book

6

7

3 Does a forced air convection oven have any advantage over a
normally heated oven? yes/no.

4 Briefly explain your answer to the previous question.

5 What advantage does a combination convection and microwave
cooker have over an ordinary microwave cooker?

6 Microwave is a method of cooking and heating food by using

_____ power.

7 A microwave oven cooks:

☐ from the outside of the food
☐ the whole food at the same time
☐ just the inside of the food
☐ only the outside of the food

8 What is the chief advantage of cooking by microwave?

9 State two advantages of the induction cooker.

1

2

10 Which is the odd one and why in relation to microwave cookery?

☐ glassware ☐ silverware ☐ plastic container
☐ paper container ☐ earthenware ☐ chinaware

11 The bratt pan may be used for five different methods of cookery:

1 2 3

4 5

12 What other advantage has the bratt pan?

13 Why is the steam jacket boiler most suitable for cooking large quantities of food with a thickened content?

14 What is the purpose of the *cool zone* in a deep fat fryer?

15 Put the names below the appropriate illustrations:

boiling pan   bratt pan   deep fat fryer
salamander   steamer   microwave oven
high pressure steamer

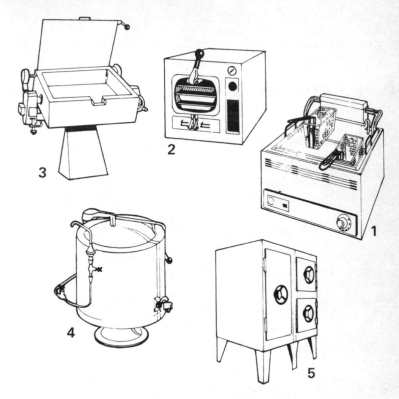

16 What is the purpose of the hot plate (hot cupboard)?

17 A bain-marie is used for:

☐ washing vegetables   ☐ basting meat
☐ keeping food hot   ☐ pot washing

18 A double sided or infra-red grill is suitable for a fast food operation: true/false.

19 Match the following:

☐ salamander   1 heat above and below
☐ grill   2 heat above
☐ contact grill   3 heat under

20 Match the following:

☐ stainless steel sink   1 general light purpose
☐ glazed earthenware sink   2 heavy pot wash
☐ galvanised iron sink   3 general purpose

21 On which of the following surfaces would you cut with a knife?

☐ wooden table   ☐ cutting board
☐ stainless steel   ☐ marble

22 Hot pans should be placed on a _____ on the table in order to protect the table surface.

23 List three points to observe when cleaning a butcher's block.

1

2

3

24 Name three factors that should influence the decision whether to use an item of mechanical equipment.

1 Can it save _____

2 Can it save _____

3 Can it produce a _____ _____ _____

25 Before loading potatoes into the potato peeler _____

and _____.

26 Name six examples of use of food mixing machine.

1   2

3   4

5   6

27 What can be the effect of overloading the mincer attachment of a food mixing machine?

28 What is the greatest potential danger to a food handler when operating a food slicing or chopping machine?

29 List five power-driven machines described as dangerous.

1   2

3   4

5

30 Working instructions should be placed in a _____ position near the machines.

31 How is milk heated in a still set?

32 The draw-off taps on coffee and milk storage chambers in still sets should be cleaned by:

☐ pushing a piece of bent wire through
☐ pushing a piece of clean muslin through
☐ using a special brush
☐ pouring through a strong detergent solution

33 In order to maintain a refrigerator at peak efficiency it should be defrosted:

☐ daily   ☐ weekly   ☐ monthly   ☐ every two months

34 Defrosting a refrigerator is necessary in order to:

☐ produce more ice cubes
☐ stop foods from freezing hard
☐ provide a supply of distilled water
☐ prevent overworking of the motor

35 Food should be tightly packed into the refrigerator in order to maximise its use: true/false.

36 Is a single temperature suitable for keeping all types of food safe and at peak condition? yes/no.

37 Why is it important to locate refrigerators away from sources of intense heat, direct sunlight and barriers to air circulation?

38 Why is it important to allow air to circulate within a refrigerator?

39 When preparing to empty and clean out a refrigerator what is the first thing to be done?

40 Refrigerators should be thoroughly cleaned inside and out at least every:

☐ 2 months ☐ 4 months ☐ 6 months

41 Defrosting a refrigerator is important because it helps equipment

perform _____ and prevents damaging build-up of

_____.

42 List two signs of an imminent breakdown in a refrigerator:

1

2

43 What are the generally recognised requirements for hygienic washing up?

A good supply of _____ water at a temperature of 60 °C

for general c_____ followed by a _____ rinse at a

temperature of 82 °C for at least _____ _____.

44 Name the three main types of dishwashing machines.

1   2   3

45 Food waste disposers are the most modern and hygienic method of waste disposal: true/false.

46 Almost every type of rubbish and swill can be finely ground down and rinsed down the drain by food waste disposers, but what are the two exceptions to this?

1   2

47 How would you prove an omelet pan?

48 Name four different types of frying pan.

1   2   3   4

49 A conical strainer is used for _____ _____ _____.

50 When is the only time that a sieve should be used upside down?

51 Rearrange the captions in correct order.

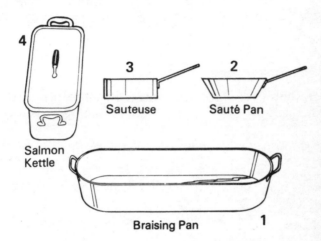

Sauteuse   Sauté Pan

Salmon Kettle

Braising Pan

52 What are the advantages of copper equipment?

53 What are the disadvantages of copper equipment?

54 Copper pans are lined with tin: true/false.

55 Give the French names for six copper pans.

1   2

3   4

5   6

56 Name two items of copper equipment that are not lined with tin.

1   2

57 ⅓ _____, ⅓_____, ⅓_____
make a paste with vinegar suitable for cleaning copper pans.

58 Why should the use of metal spoons or whisks be avoided with aluminium pans?

59 Is water boiled in aluminium pans suitable for making tea? yes/no.

60 Is stainless steel a good conductor of heat?

61 Why do some stainless steel pans have a thick layer of copper in the base?

62 Non-stick pans are best cleaned with:

☐ wire wool   ☐ kitchen paper
☐ Brillo pad   ☐ cleaning powder

63 State the most suitable material from which each of these utensils should be made.

Friture   Conical Strainer   Mushroom   Sugar Boiler

64 What four points should be observed in order to prevent warping and splintering of cutting boards?

1

2

3

4

65 Name three materials from which piping bags are made.

1   2   3

8

Gas, electricity and water

Gas

pages 243–251

1 Write the method of transferring heat under the appropriate diagram.

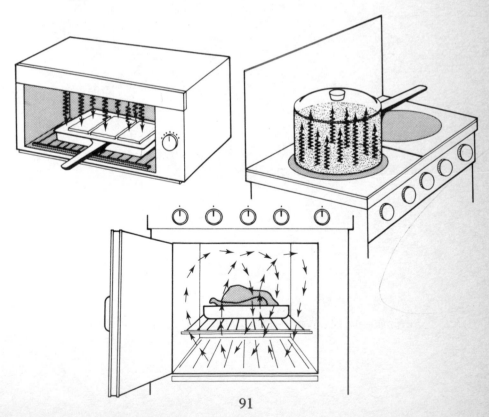

2   In the calculation of gas bills British Gas states the c_____
    v_____ of the gas in b_____ t_____ u_____.

3   What is the purpose of a thermostat?
    ☐ To ignite the main jet
    ☐ To control the pilot
    ☐ To admit the air
    ☐ To control the temperature

4   **a** The action of a rod-type thermostat depends upon the fact that
    some metals expand more than others when heated: true/false.

    b The action of a liquid thermostat depends upon the fact that a
    vapour expands when heated: true/false.

5   Does air rise on being heated?

6   For what reason would Calor Gas be used?

7   Give an example of when it is extensively used.

Electricity

pages 252–262

1   Which of the following are insulators?
    ☐ rubber   ☐ metal   ☐ plastic
    ☐ glass   ☐ tap water   ☐ porcelain

2   The pressure of flow of electricity is measured by

    _____.

3   The rate of flow of electrical current is measured by _____

4   The resistance of wires to the passage of electricity is measured by

    _____.

5   To cut off the entire lighting or power circuit you would:

☐ phone the Electricity Board
☐ pull out all plugs and turn out all lights
☐ pull down the main switch
☐ sever the wires at the meter

6   Read this meter:

7   A fuse acts as a s_____ d_____.

8   Indicate which of the following cause blown fuses:

☐ too many appliances plugged into a circuit
☐ using a 5 amp fuse on a lighting circuit
☐ plugging a fire into a light socket
☐ using a 10 amp fuse for an electric iron
☐ short circuit due to insulation failure
☐ switching off at the main suddenly

9   When preparing a fuse the first thing to do is:

☐ stand on a non-conductor
☐ turn off the main switch
☐ phone for the electrician
☐ turn off the appliance
☐ put on rubber gloves

10   When wiring a 13 amp plug, match

☐ green/yellow	1 live
☐ brown	2 neutral
☐ blue	3 earth

11 An absorption-type refrigerator has moving parts: true/false.

12 Deep-freezers should maintain temperatures of:

☐ $-19\,°C$
☐ $-18\,°C$
☐ $-15\,°C$
☐ $-13\,°C$

13 What percentage of the total energy used in the United Kingdom per year is accounted for by the hotel and catering industry?

☐ 0·3%   ☐ 1·3%   ☐ 2·3%
☐ 3·0%   ☐ 3·3%

14 With moderate improvements in efficiency and some rationalisation in the use of equipment what is the estimated overall saving per year the hotel and catering industry could achieve?

☐ 2%   ☐ 12%   ☐ 15%
☐ 20%   ☐ 30%

15 What would be the value in pounds per year of the saving in the previous question?

☐ 5 million   ☐ 8·7 million   ☐ 10·5 million
☐ 12 million   ☐ 15·6 million

16 Give two examples of energy wastage in the use of kitchen equipment.

1

2

17 Describe two examples of energy saving equipment.

1

2

Water

pages 262–276

1 Wholesome water is free from

    1   2

    3   4

2 Water in certain districts is described as being hard.
Temporary hardness is caused by c_____ or
m_____ b_____.
Permanent hardness is caused by s_____ or
c_____ of c_____ and m_____.

3 The Water Board's stopcock is situated:
    ☐ in the cistern   ☐ in the roof
    ☐ inside the premises   ☐ outside the premises

4 When the ball arm of a ball valve lowers does it open or close the valve?

5 Flushing cisterns should discharge:
    ☐ 1 gallon of water in 2 seconds
    ☐ 2 gallons of water in 5 seconds
    ☐ 5 gallons of water in 2 seconds
    ☐ 2 gallons of water in 1 second

6   Name the parts indicated by arrows.

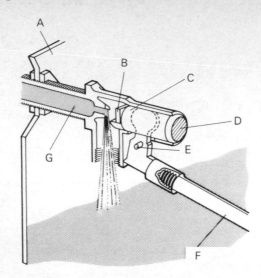

7   Washers for modern taps are obtainable in how many sizes?

☐ 1   ☐ 2   ☐ 3   ☐ 4

8   The *stop-cock* is also called the:

☐ ball-valve   ☐ stop-valve
☐ stop-pipe

9   Why does the cold water flow into the bottom of the hot water
storage tank?

10   An immersion heater may be connected to either the electricity or
gas supply: true/false.

11   To clear a blocked sink, use a:

☐ rubber water plunger   ☐ spider
☐ jelly bag   ☐ waste master

12   When water freezes it _____.

13   What is the reason for lagging water-pipes?

9

Kitchen organisation and supervision

pages 277–292

1   What points affect the organisation of the kitchen?

2   State four responsibilities of the Head Chef or Head Cook.

   1

   2

   3

   4

3   What is the French for the *Second Chef*?

4   A *Chef de partie* is in charge of

   ☐ the food for small parties of customers
   ☐ a section of the work in the kitchen
   ☐ banquets, buffets and parties
   ☐ the menus for all functions

5 In the traditional organisation what were the responsibilities of the

1 larder chef

2 pastry

3 sauce chef

4 relief chef?

6 What does the word *commis* indicate?

7 Give a definition of *entrées*.

8 What is the name given to the chef responsible for the entrées?

9 Which partie cooks the grilled and deep fried foods?

10 What is the French name for the *fish cook*?

11 Yorkshire pudding is made by the:

☐ vegetable cook   ☐ relief cook
☐ pastry cook   ☐ roast cook

12 What does the aboyeur do?

☐ act as toastmaster
☐ call out the orders
☐ carve the joints in the room
☐ look after the still room

13 Name four subsidiary departments of the kitchen

1   2

3   4

14 What are the advantages of an operation where the kitchen is on full view to the customers?

15 What effects have the continually increasing costs of space, equipment, maintenance, fuel and labour had on the organisation of the kitchen?

16 Name the person who introduced the *partie* system.

17 The variety and number of dishes on the menu does not affect the organisation of the kitchen: true/false.

18 Give three examples of situations where large numbers of people need to be served food at the same time.

   1

   2

   3

19 State the major advantage of the cook-freeze system.

20 Good supervision is the effective use of:
   1 m_____   2 m_____   3 m_____

21 State the three functions of a supervisor.

   1

   2

   3

22 A supervisor needs to be able t_____ d_____ as well as knowing h_____ t_____ d_____.

23 Give an example of why a supervisor needs to forecast and plan.

24 Complete the following:

Organising consists of ensuring that w_____ is wanted, is w_____ it is wanted, w_____ it is wanted in the r_____ amount at the r_____ time.

25 Delegation is an important aspect of supervision: true/false.

26 A good supervisor:

☐ creates problems
☐ makes problems
☐ anticipates problems
☐ causes problems

27 Tick those qualities which an effective supervisor needs:

☐ good communicator
☐ tactless
☐ impetuous
☐ possesses technical knowledge
☐ organising ability
☐ understanding of people
☐ motivator
☐ disciplinarian

28 An example of social influence on the catering industry would be

29 Tick those items which could be described as having an economic effect on the catering industry.

☐ unemployment   ☐ a very wet summer
☐ rail strike   ☐ a decrease in VAT

10

Food production systems

pages 293–310

1   Specify six problem areas in the industry which may be partially solved by having a food production system:

1   2

3   4

5   6

2   Very briefly explain:

1 *cook-chill*

2 *cook-freeze*

3 *sous-vide*

3   Between what temperatures should cook-chill foods be stored?

4   The term for reheating cook-chill food is:

☐ regeneration   ☐ remuneration
☐ renovation   ☐ restoration

5   What is the difference between making sauces for cook-freeze and those for cook-chill?

6 When several kitchens are supplied from a main kitchen for heating frozen foods, they are called:

☐ peramateur
☐ peripheral
☐ spherical

7 List eight benefits of a cook-chill/cook-freeze system:

1   2

3   4

5   6

7   8

8 State four advantages of cook-freeze over cook-chill:

1   2

3   4

9 State six advantages of cook-chill over cook-freeze:

1   2

3   4

5   6

10 What is the most important factor to be considered with either system.

11 What is the function of a bacteriologist or microbiologist?

12 Describe the pouches used for sous-vide.

13 State four advantages and four disadvantages of the sous-vide system:

Advantages

1   2

3   4

Disadvantages

1   2

3   4

14 What is a *centralised production unit*?

15 What kinds of staff are required in a central food production system?

11

Health and safety

pages 311–331

1 Briefly state the two aims of the Health and Safety at Work Act.

  1

  2

2 At work every employee must take reasonable care of himself or herself and who else?

3 Regarding safety at work, an employee must not interfere with what?

4 An employee should cooperate with whom at all times.

5 Whose function is it to improve the existing standards of hygiene, to act as an adviser and to enforce the hygiene laws?

6 State three ways in which accidents can be caused in the kitchen

  1   2   3

7 During a busy kitchen service, the golden rule is 'never run': true/false.

8 Why may a blunt knife be more likely to cause an accident than a sharp one?

9 State five safety rules to be observed when handling knives.

1

2

3

4

5

10 What is the most important safety precaution to observe when cleaning a cutting machine?

11 Why should guards be in place when using machines?
- ☐ To do the work more quickly
- ☐ To prevent the operator being injured
- ☐ To deter stealing
- ☐ To stop food being spilled

12 Why should frozen meat be thawed before being boned?

13 If you cut your hand with a fish bone it may turn s_____.

14 A burn is caused by

15 A scald is caused by

16 When an accident occurs who must be informed?
- ☐ the Police
- ☐ the hospital
- ☐ the employer
- ☐ the health officer

17 The sensible length to wear an apron in the kitchen is
- ☐ ankle length
- ☐ justbelow the crutch
- ☐ justbelow the knees
- ☐ under the arms and around the waist

18 When working over the stove is it sensible to have the jacket/overall sleeves rolled up or down?

19 Tick the essential points for an oven cloth:

□ wet   □ thin   □ torn
□ thick   □ dry   □ with holes

20 When shallow frying, in which direction is the food put into the pan and why?

21 If foods are tipped out of the frying basket into the friture, a

_____ must be at hand.

22 To mark the handle or lid or a HOT pan you would:

□ write on it the word hot in flour
□ place a piece of red paper on it
□ put the burn ointment beside it
□ sprinkle a little flour on it

23 The correct amount of fat in a movable friture for safety purposes is:

□ ⅔ full   □ ½ full   □ ¼ full   □ ¾ full

24 Wet foods should be d_____ and d_____ before being placed in hot fat.

25 Should the fat in a movable friture bubble over on to a gas stove, you would first:

□ call your immediate superior
□ call the kitchen porter
□ lift out the food with a spider
□ turn off the gas tap

26 When using a mixing machine with a blade, whisk or hook, what is the essential safety precaution that you should observe?

27 State five safety rules to be observed when using machinery.

1   2   3

4   5

28 A gas explosion can be caused in the kitchen because:

☐ there is no pilot
☐ the gas is turned off at the main
☐ the main jet has not ignited from the pilot
☐ the gas has not been turned on

29 It is not necessary to mop up water spilt on to a kitchen floor as the heat of the kitchen will do this fairly quickly: true/false.

30 Why should containers containing liquid never be put above eye-level?

☐ other persons not aware that they contain liquid
☐ liquid above eye-level is difficult to control
☐ containers above eye-level are heavier
☐ liquid in the container moves more when above eye-level

31 State four signs indicating that a person is suffering from shock.

1

2

3

4

32 What is the first-aid treatment for a cut?

☐ sprinkle it with salt in order to disinfect it
☐ give a glass of brandy
☐ wash the skin around the cut and apply a waterproof dressing
☐ wrap it in a tea-towel and send for the doctor

33 If breathing has stopped, a_____ r_____ must be started before any other treatment is given.

34 Slight burns or scalds should be immersed in:

☐ iced water   ☐ hot running water
☐ warmwater   ☐ cold running water

35 In cases of electric shock, firstly:

- ☐ give the person a glass of water
- ☐ switch off the current
- ☐ apply artificial respiration
- ☐ send for a doctor

36 State three signs which may indicate a person is about to faint.

1   2   3

37 Name two common causes of fire in a catering establishment.

1   2

38 Indicate the correct procedures in the event of a fire in the kitchen.

- ☐ Turn off gas and electricity
- ☐ Close doors and windows
- ☐ Run out of the kitchen
- ☐ Turn off fans
- ☐ Warn people in the vicinity of the fire
- ☐ Shout in a loud voice 'Fire, don't panic!'
- ☐ Use appropriate extinguishers
- ☐ Call fire brigade

39 If a fire is spreading in the kitchen, what should be done to doors and windows?

40 Match the appropriate extinguisher with the type of fire.

1 Fire blanket   2 Foam   3 Dry powder

Fire caused by fat	
Electrical fire	
Person's clothing on fire	

41   Complete this fire triangle with one word.

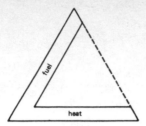

42   To remove the fuel is to _____ the fire.

To remove the air is to _____ the fire.

To remove the heat is to _____ the fire.

43   Match these colours to types of fire extinguishers:

blue _____   black _____

red _____   cream _____

green _____

44   What do you understand by a good *mise-en-place*?

45   Place the following in order to show an efficient flow of work when making croquette potatoes:

breadcrumbs   egg wash   flour   duchess potato mixture

46   Why is it desirable to have a planned layout when working?

47   Which is the best working method for a right-handed person?

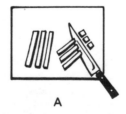

A   B   C

48 A skilled craftsman achieves a high standard of work with the:

☐ least effort
☐ most effort
☐ great effort
☐ considerable effort

49 State three savings that can be made to reduce wastage by studying working methods.

1

2

3

50 In addition to paying attention to good working habits, it is desirable to:

☐ cultivate the right attitude to work
☐ to take 'short cuts' and finish early
☐ to work as fast as possible, irrespective of result
☐ to adopt an attitude of not accepting advice

12

Hygiene

Personal hygiene

pages 332–339

1 S_____ respect is necessary in every food handler because

2 Personal cleanliness is essential to prevent g_____ getting on to food.

3 Give another word for *germs*.

4 Hands must be thoroughly washed frequently, particularly

5 Why is jewellery not worn in the kitchen?

6 Which of the following statements is correct?

When handling food you should use:

☐ fresh-coloured nail varnish
☐ pink nail varnish
☐ no nail varnish

7 Why should finger nails be kept short when handling food?

8 List the faults in personal hygiene shown below.

9 When handling food, hair should be covered:

☐ because of the appearance of the worker
☐ because of the legal requirements
☐ to keep customers happy
☐ because of hygienic reasons

10 Why are paper handkerchiefs or tissues preferable to linen or cotton handkerchiefs?

11 Why is it important not to sneeze over people, food or working surfaces?

12 Sound teeth are essential to good health: true/false.

13 You should visit the dentist:

☐ every 5 years
☐ every 3 years
☐ every 3–6 months
☐ when you have toothache

14 When tasting food which should you use?

☐ wooden spoon
☐ teaspoon
☐ your finger
☐ ladle

15 Indicate with arrows where bacteria will be found in large numbers.

16 Cuts, burns, scratches and similar openings in the skin are best covered with:

☐ clean gauze
☐ clean bandage
☐ waterproof dressing
☐ antiseptic ointment

17 Explain two ways in which germs may be transferred on to food by someone smoking in the kitchen.

1

2

18 Spitting is an objectionable habit which should never occur, but why is this?

19 Where should outdoor clothing, and other clothing which has been taken off before wearing whites, be kept?

20 What is wrong with this picture of a food handler regarding safety and hygiene?

1   2   3

21 List four essential points to ensure good health and physical fitness.

1   2

3   4

22 When working in a hot kitchen and perspiring freely, the ideal way to replace liquid lost is by

☐ taking salt tablets   ☐ taking glucose tablets
☐ drinking pure water   ☐ drinking beer

23 Why should picking of food be discouraged?

24 Match the following important points for kitchen clothing:

☐ Protective
☐ Washable
☐ Suitable colour
☐ Lightweight
☐ Strong
☐ Absorbent

1 to be comfortable in a hot atmosphere
2 to enable perspiration to be soaked up
3 need to withstand hard wear
4 so as to indicate the need to be washed
5 because of the need for frequent change
6 to prevent excessive heat affecting the body

25 List the errors you note in this illustration of a cook in the kitchen.

26 To which three groups of people is kitchen hygiene particularly important?

1   2   3

Kitchen hygiene

pages 340–346

1 Windows in the kitchen used for ventilation should be screened to prevent the entry of dust, insects and birds: true/false.

2 The most suitable surface for kitchen floors is:

☐ rubber tiles ☐ lino tiles
☐ quarry tiles ☐ concrete

3 State five important factors of kitchen wall surfaces.

1   2   3

4   5

4 Name three items of kitchen equipment which are difficult to clean and state how you would clean them.

1

2

3

5 When cleaning large equipment such as electrical mixers, slicers etc, what should be done first?

6 Failure to maintain equipment and utensils hygienically and in good repair may cause food _____.

7 Why should you not wash aluminium saucepans in water containing soda?

8 Why should tinned lined saucepans be dried after being washed?

9 Hygiene is the study of h_____ and the prevention of d_____.

10 Numer in order of importance:

☐ Having the right attitude to hygiene
☐ Seeing films on hygiene
☐ Reading books on hygiene
☐ Practising hygienic habits
☐ Attending lectures on hygiene

11 Food handlers should not only know the Food Hygiene Regulations, but should practise them in their daily work: true/false.

12 In a catering establishment can any of the following be excused in relation to hygiene? Neglect, ignorance, thoughtlessness, low standard, poor facilities: yes/no.

13 The average number of notified cases of food poisoning each year over the past ten years has been

☐ 400   ☐ 8000
☐ 4000   ☐ 14000

Food hygiene

pages 347–371

1 What is *food poisoning*?

2 List eight ways to prevent food poisoning.

1	2
3	4
5	6
7	8

3 By far the greatest number of cases of food poisoning are caused by harmful _____.

4   Food contaminated by _____ is by far the most common cause of food poisoning.

5   What have the following in common?

zinc   rhubarb leaves   lead   arsenic

6   By what means can chemical food poisoning be avoided?

7   What word means the same as *poison*?

8   Bacteria which form spores can withstand h_____ for long

p_____ of t_____.

9   Because bacteria multiply by dividing in two under suitable conditions, one bacterium could multiply in 10–12 hours to between:

☐ 100–200 thousand   ☐ 100–200 million
☐ 400–500 thousand   ☐ 500–1000 million

10 Typhoid, paratyphoid and dysentery are known as f_____

b_____ diseases.

11 For the multiplication of bacteria certain conditions are necessary.

1 _____ of the right kind

2 _____ must be adequate

3 _____ must be suitable

4 _____ must elapse

12 Are bacteria killed by cold? yes/no.

13 Which of these foods are most easily contaminated?

Pork Pie   Trifle   Pickled Onions   Salt Beef

14 In which of the following should food not be stored and why?

☐ larder   ☐ refrigerator   ☐ store   ☐ kitchen

15 Why should food be kept in a cool larder or refrigerator?

16 Which of the following provides an ideal heat for bacteria to grow?

☐ cold soup   ☐ lukewarm soup
☐ hot soup   ☐ boiling soup

17 State the temperatures between which bacteria multiply rapidly:

_____ and _____

18 Will bacteria remain dormant for long periods? yes/no

19 If foods have been contaminated before being made cold and kept in the refrigerator, on raising the temperature by keeping the foods in the kitchen for a period of time the bacteria will

_____.

20 Bacteria require moisture for growth, they cannot multiply on dry food: true/false.

21 List four foods ideal for the growth of bacteria.

1   2   3   4

22 Indicate the foods which need the greatest care to prevent food poisoning.

☐ gravy   ☐ milk   ☐ dried peas   ☐ jelly
☐ cream   ☐ tea leaves   ☐ aspic   ☐ flour

23 *Salmonella* is the name of:

☐ a patent fly catcher
☐ the scientist who discovered food poisoning
☐ living food poisoning bacteria
☐ an insect spray fitted in kitchens

24 *Clostridium Welchii* is now called

☐ perfection
☐ perfringens
☐ ferpingons
☐ ferfringens

25 Explain the danger to humans of flies landing on food.

26 What is wrong and why?

Raw chicken

Cooked meat

27 Germs present on human hands and other parts of the skin and in the nose or throat or sores and spots are S_____.

28 Food poisoning bacteria live in:

1 the s_____

2 h_____

3 a_____, i_____ and b_____

29 To prevent food poisoning those concerned with food must stop bacteria from _____ and stop them from _____.

30 With what types of food poisoning are the following associated?

Flies

Insects

31 What is the responsibility of the carrier of an infectious disease?

32 Indicate how infection can be spread by:

1 humans

2 animals, insects, birds

3 inanimate objects (tea-towels, bowls, etc.)

33 The cook's best friend in the kitchen is a cat or small dog as they will help to kill the rats and mice. Discuss briefly.

34 State six ways to prevent infestation from vermin.

1   2

3   4

5   6

35 One of the most important ways to prevent contamination of food is by the correct _____ of food.

36 When cleaning pans used for porridge or starchy foods they should be:

☐ soaked in cold water
☐ soaked in warm water
☐ soaked in salt water
☐ soaked in hot water

37 The temperature of washing up water should be:

☐ 62 °C   ☐ 72 °C   ☐ 82 °C   ☐ 92 °C

38 In which months of the year is extra care needed when storing foods?

39 What is wrong in this diagram?

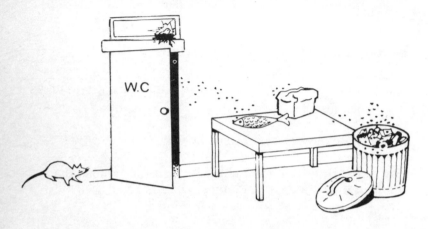

40 Why may some shell fish, such as oysters and mussels, cause food poisoning?

41 Which sauce made with eggs is liable to cause food poisoning? Describe briefly how this can happen.

42 *Rechauffé* indicates what kind of dish?

43 Milk to be safe should be:

☐ pasteurised   ☐ pacified
☐ pasturised   ☐ patronised

44 Name four made-up food dishes that require extra care in their preparation

1   2

3   4

45 Tinned hams should be stored in the refrigerator: true/false.

46 Why should boned and rolled joints of meat require extra care in cooking?

47 Pork should always be well cooked: true/false.

48 Explain the reason for your answer to the previous question.

49 Why do made-up fish dishes require special care and attention?

50 Why must watercress be thoroughly washed?

51 When handling left-over foods for re-use, if in doubt as to their freshness, what golden rule should you follow?

52 To whom should an employer report a case of typhoid?

53 List two items which should be available near to hand basins in kitchens?

1   2

54 Copies of the Food Hygiene Regulations may be obtained from HM _____ Office.

55 What is the penalty for any person found guilty of an offence under the Food Hygiene Regulations?

56 Name two institutions concerned with health and hygiene.

1

2

13

Elementary nutrition and food science

pages 372–395

1   Give a brief definition of food.

2   List the six nutrients.

1 carbohydrates   2 protein

3 vitamins   4 minerals

5 ~~fibre~~ water   6 fats

3   The study of nutrients is known as _nutrition_ .

4   Which food contains only one nutrient?

☐ egg   ☑ sugar
☐ apple   ☐ flour

5   For the body to obtain maximum benefit from food it is essential
    that everyone concerned with the buying, storage, cooking and
    serving of food and the compiling of menus should have some

    knowledge of _nutrition_ .

6   Digestion is the _breaking down_ of the _food_ .

7   Digestion takes place in the mouth where s_saliva___ is added, in the stomach where g_astric___. j_uices___ are added and in the small intestine where the n_utrients__ are broken down further and additional j_uices___ are added.

8   To enable the body to benefit from food it must be absorbed into the blood stream: true/false. _T_

9   When does absorption take place?
    ☐ When drinking with food
    ☐ At the same time as digestion
    ☑ After the food has been broken down
    ☐ Just before digestion

10 If the body is to obtain full benefit from foods, then the foods must s_mell___, l_ook___ and taste attractive.

11 What do you understand by a *state of malnutrition*?
    lacking in one or more of the major nutrients

12 Rearrange the following tables of the main functions of nutrients correctly.

Energy	Growth and repair	Regulation of body processes
Proteins	Water _Protein_	Minerals
Fats	Carbohydrates	Proteins _Vit_
Vitamins	Minerals	Water
Carbohydrate		

13 Name the two kinds of protein.
    1 _animal_   2 _veg_

14 Protein is needed for _growth___ of the body and for the _repair___ of body tissues.

15 Do growing children and expectant mothers need more protein than other adults? yes/no. _Y_

126

16 Explain the reason for your answer to the previous question.

growing + high energy

17 List four foods that give the main supply of protein in the average diet.

1 *cheese.*   2 *poultry*

3 *fish.*   4 *eggs.*

18 Protein is composed of ___*amino*___ acids.

19 All these acids are essential to the body: true/false.   *F*

20 The protein of cheese is different from the protein of meat because the arrangement of the ___*amino acids*___ is not the same.

21 Which is the odd one out and why?

onion - to add flavour

22 Moderately cooked protein is most easy to digest: true/false.

T

23 Give an example to illustrate your answer to the previous question. *eggs.*

24 What are the two main groups of fats? *animal + veg.*

25 The function of fats is to:

1 protect vital ___*organs*___ of the body

2 provide heat and ___*energy*___

3 in the case of certain fats provide ___*vitamins*___

127

26 Indicate the origin of the following foods by writing A for animal and V for vegetable.

☒ butter	☑ soya bean	☑ olive oil	☒ herring
☒ cod liver oil	☒ suet	☒ meat fat	☒ cream
☑ margarine	☑ nuts	☒ lard	☒ dripping
☑ sunflower oil	☒ bacon	☒ halibut liver oil	☒ cheese

27 Olive oil is a fat which is liquid at room temperature: true/false.

T

28 Which is the odd one out and why?

Herring   Walnuts   Olives   Black Currants   Avocado Pear

doesn't contain fat.

29 Fats differ because of the ___fatty___ acids from which they are derived.

30 Give three examples of fatty acids.

1 butyric.   2 oleic

3 stearic

31 Fatty acids affect the _____ and _____ of the fat.

32 Fats provide the body with _____ and _____.

33 List six oily fish.

1   2

3   4

5   6

34 Name the three main groups of carbohydrates.

1   2   3

35 The function of carbohydrates is to provide the body with most of its:

☐ vitamins   ☐ carbon
☐ protection   ☐ energy

36 Name three foods which are main suppliers of carbohydrate in the diet.

1   2   3

37 Sugar is the simplest form of carbohydrate: true/false.

38 Match the following:

☒ maltose   1 beet and cane sugar
☒ lactose   2 fruit
☒ sucrose   3 milk
☒ glucose   4 honey and animal blood
☒ fructose   5 grain

39 Which of the following foods contribute starch to the diet?

☐ rice   ☐ peas
☐ beef   ☐ butter beans
☐ flour   ☐ onions
☐ plaice   ☐ apples

40 Give three examples of foods containing starch in each of the following categories.

Whole grains	1	2	3
Powdered grains	1	2	3
Vegetables	1	2	3
Unripe fruit	1	2	3
Cereals	1	2	3
Cooked starch	1	2	3
Pasta	1	2	3

41 Cellulose is the:

☐ skin of fresh fish   ☐ coarser structure of vegetables and
☐ sinew of meat   cereals
                        ☐ most complex of all the vitamins

42 What is the purpose of cellulose in the diet?

43   Which is the odd one out and why?

44   Vitamins are the chemical substances which are _____ for life.

45   Vitamins are produced both naturally and synthetically: true/false.

46   Give two examples of the general function of vitamins.

1   2

47   In which of the following is Vitamin A found?

☐ liver   ☐ cooking fat ☐ carrots   ☐ cauliflower
☐ lamb   ☐ herrings   ☐ apricots   ☐ milk
☐ butter   ☐ plaice   ☐ cheese   ☐ cherries

48   Vitamin A is fat soluble: true/false.

49   List three functions of vitamins.

1   2   3

50   Which vitamin is necessary for healthy bones and teeth?

51   Which two vitamins are added to margarine?

1   2

52   Name the most important source of vitamin D.

53   Name three groups of foods containing vitamin D.

1   2   3

54   Is vitamin B required to enable the body to obtain energy from
      the carbohydrates? yes/no.

55   Name three foods in which vitamin B is found:
      1   2   3

56   List the three main substances which make up the vitamin B
      group.
      1   2   3

57   Can vitamin B be lost in cooking? yes/no.

58   Indicate by using initials which of the following foods are sources
      of B1 Thiamine (T), Riboflavine (R) or Niacin (N).

      ☐ wholemeal   ☐ bacon   ☐ yeast   ☐ oatmeal
         bread   ☐ liver   ☐ meat extract   ☐ beef
      ☐ cheese   ☐ kidney   ☐ peas   ☐ brewers'
      ☐ eggs   yeast

59   What is another name for *Niacin*?

60   Vitamin C can be lost in cooking and by bad s_____.

61   Name six foods containing vitamin C.
      1   2   3

      4   5   6

62   Match the following:
      ☐ egg yolk   1 vitamin A
      ☐ kidney   2 vitamin B
      ☐ oranges   3 vitamin C
      ☐ yeast   4 vitamin D

63   Which three of the following mineral elements are most likely to
      be deficient in the diet?

      ☐ calcium   ☐ phosphorus   ☐ iron
      ☐ sodium   ☐ potassium   ☐ iodine

131

64 List three sources of each of the mineral elements selected in the previous question.

Mineral element   *Source 1*   *Source 2*   *Source 3*

65 The use that the body makes of calcium is dependent upon the presence of vitamin _____.

66 Name two foods that are sources of calcium.

1 MILK.   2 EGGS

67 What is the mineral element needed particularly for growing bones and teeth for expectant and nursing mothers?

68 The body makes use of phosphorus in conjunction with c_Alcium__ and vitamin ___B___.

69 Which four of the following foods are sources of phosphorus?

☐ liver   ☐ eggs   ☐ fish
☐ cheese   ☐ lettuce   ☐ spinach

70 Iron is required for building the haemoglobin in blood and is therefore necessary for transporting _____ and _____ _____ round the body.

71 Which three of the following foods are sources of iron?

☐ lean meat   ☐ offal   ☐ egg yolk
☐ tomatoes   ☐ carrots   ☐ cream

72 Which mineral element is found in all body fluids and is found as salt?

132

73 Which mineral element do we lose from the body when we perspire?

74 Water is required for which body functions?

M_____ B_____ F_____

A_____ E_____

D_____ S_____

75 Excluding liquids, name six foods that contain water.

1   2   3

4   5   6

76 Match the following:

☐ protein   1 nutritive value not affected by normal
☐ carbohydrate   cooking
☐ fat   2 lost by cooking and keeping hot
                       3 destroyed by high temperature and use of
☐ iron   bicarbonate soda
☐ vitamin B1   4 may be acquired from pans in which
☐ vitamin C   cooked
                       5 needs to be thoroughly cooked
                       6 overcooking reduces nutritive value

77 What effect does overcooking have on the nutritive value of food?

78 Unless starch is thoroughly cooked it cannot be properly digested: true/false.

79 Is the nutritive value of fat affected by cooking? yes/no.

80 Which of the following vitamins can withstand cooking temperatures and are not lost in cooking?

Vitamins   ☐ A   ☐ B   ☐ C   ☐ D

81 Why is energy required by the body?

133

82 Foods containing a high fat content will have a high _____ content.

Foods containing a lot of water will have a low _____ content.

83 By which term is the energy value of food measured?

☐ calcium   ☐ celanus
☐ calcius   ☐ calorie

84 People engaged in energetic work require more calories than people engaged in sedentary occupations: true/false.

85 Who needs the highest daily calorie intake?

☐ a young male apprentice aged 19 playing football two evenings a week
☐ a young lady receptionist who attends a disco once a week
☐ an office typist who is a keen television fan
☐ an accountant who is studying hard for examinations

86 _____ is said to be the almost perfect food.

87 Why is margarine sometimes more nutritious than butter?

88 Why is the food value of cheese exceptional?

89 What does bacon contain nutritionally that is not present in other meats?

90 Cheaper cuts of meat are less nourishing than dearer cuts of meat: true/false.

91 Sweetbreads are valuable to invalids because they

☐ look appetising   ☐ are easily digested
☐ are very tasty   ☐ are highly nutritious

92 When bones of tinned salmon or sardines are eaten, they are a source of calcium: true/false.

93   Which of the following is correct?

☐ Fish is a more valuable source of protein than meat
☐ Fish is equally valuable as a source of protein as meat
☐ Fish is a less valuable source of protein than meat
☐ Fish is not a source of protein at all

94   The oil in oily fish is contained in the liver: true/false.

95   The carbohydrate in unripe fruit is in the form of ＿＿＿＿＿
which changes to ＿＿＿＿＿ when the fruit is ripe.

96   Which is the odd one out and why?

☐ oranges   ☐ lemons   ☐ strawberries
☐ blackcurrants ☐ pears   ☐ grapefruit

97   Nuts are a source of cellulose: true/false.

98   Green vegetables are valuable because they contain which of the
following vitamins and minerals?

☐ iron, calcium, vitamins A and C
☐ phosphorus, calcium, vitamins A and D
☐ iron, calcium, vitamins B and C
☐ iodine, sodium, vitamins A and D

99   Potatoes are a valuable source of vitamin D because they are
eaten in large quantities: true/false.

100 State the main value of onions in cookery.

101 Which vitamin is contained in wholemeal flour?

102 Saccharine has no food value: true/false.

103 What food value have tea and coffee?

104 When compiling a balanced diet, in which order are the
following considered?

☐ body building foods
☐ energy producing foods
☐ protective foods

14

Preservation of foods

pages 396–405

1 In the air there are certain micro-organisms which cause food to go bad, called m_____, y_____, b_____.

2 When whiskers form on food they are called _____.

3 On which three foods are whiskers likely to grow?
   1   2   3

4 Are all the micro-organisms destructive? yes/no.

5 Most micro-organisms can be checked by r_____ and killed by h_____.

6 Explain the reason for your answer to the previous question.

7 Dry foods and those containing a high percentage of sugar or vinegar are less likely to go bad: true/false.

8 Enzymes are chemical substances produced by living cells: true/false.

9 Fruits are ripened by the action of

10 When meat is hung it becomes tender due to

136

11 If enzyme activity goes too far foods can be spoiled: true/false.

13 To prevent enzyme activity going too far, foods must be

r_____ or heated to a high t_____.

14 Which is the correct way to write the term for the degree of acidity of a food material?

☐ pH   ☐ HP   ☐ Ph   ☐ ph

15 What number of the range of acidity and alkaninity would you give to

lemons _____,   butter _____,   egg white _____.

16 The browning of cut apples and bananas is caused by enzymes: true/false.

17 What is the effect of lemon juice on cut bananas and apples?

18 Name eight ways of preserving food.

1   2

3   4

5   6

7   8

19 Drying and dehydration of food is achieved by extracting the m_____ from the food.

20 The drying of foods prevents the growth of m_____,
y_____ and b_____.

21 Originally foods were dried in the sun: true/false.

22 What is the modern process of freezing and drying?

☐ accelerated freeze drying
☐ quick frozen drying
☐ deep frozen drying
☐ frozen and dried

23 Give three advantages of dried food:

1

2

3

24 Name six foods preserved by drying

1   2

3   4

5   6

25 Little flavour or food value is lost in the drying of food: true/false.

26 Which is the odd one out and why?

☐ currants   ☐ sultanas   ☐ prunes
☐ strawberries   ☐ apricots

27 Can eggs and milk be dried? yes/no.

28 Explain in a *few* words the roller and the spray processes.

29 Are micro-organisms in food killed by refrigeration? yes/no.

30 Cold storage of fresh foods retards the decay of food, it does not prevent it from going bad: true/false.

31 Quick freezing is satisfactory because:

☐ medium ice crystals are formed in the food cells
☐ large ice crystals are formed in the food cells
☐ small ice crystals are formed in the food cells
☐ small ice crystals are formed outside the food cells

32 Meat kept in a temperature just above freezing point is known as

c_____ meat.

33 The meat referred to in the previous question will keep for up to

☐ 1 month   ☐ 3 months
☐ 2 months   ☐ 6 months

34 Why are lamb carcasses frozen but not beef carcasses?

35 Both raw and cooked meats can be quick frozen: true/false.

36 State four advantages for using frozen raw foods.

1

2

3

4

37 State four advantages for using pre-cooked frozen foods.

1

2

3

4

38 What is meant by a 'blown' can?

☐ one that has a slight dent
☐ one that has no label
☐ one that had air blown in during processing
☐ one with a bulge at either end

39 What should be done with blown cans?

40 Where is the correct place to store tinned ham?

☐ in the deep freeze
☐ in the refrigerator
☐ in the larder
☐ a cool part of the kitchen

41 Tinned food will keep indefinitely: true/false.

42 List the following can sizes in order of size – largest first.

 A2   A10   14Z   A1   A2½

43 What is the advantage of preserving meat and fish by salting and smoking?

44 Name two meats preserved by salting or pickling.

1   2

45 In what is meat pickled?

☐ brine   ☐ vinaigrette
☐ vinegar   ☐ spiced vinegar

46 Name four fish preserved by salting and pickling.

1   2

3   4

47 What is brine?

☐ stock containing saltpetre
☐ water containing iron
☐ a salt court bouillon
☐ a salt solution

48 What is the effect of adding salt to butter and margarine?

49 Name four items preserved because of the sugar content.

1   2

3   4

50 If too little sugar is used when making jam, what will be the effect on the keeping quality?

51 Name six foods preserved in vinegar.

1   2

3   4

5   6

52 Match the item with a method of preservation.

☐ glacé   1 salmon
☐ crystallised   2 peel
☐ candied   3 onions
☐ pickled   4 angelica
☐ smoked   5 sultanas
☐ dried   6 cherries

53 Name a substitute for wheat flour for use in thickening foods to be deep-frozen.

54 The nutritional value of foods such as texturised vegetable protein should be:

☐ not more than the natural food it simulates
☐ less the natural food it simulates
☐ considerably less than the natural food it simulates
☐ equal to the natural food it simulates

15

Service of food

pages 406–413

1 State four varied types of food service:

   1

   2

   3

   4

2 Which method of food service is the most expensive to operate?

3 Explain briefly why kitchen staff should appreciate the problems of waiting staff.

4 State four points to be considered for the benefit of both the waiter and the customer when plating or dishing food:

   1

   2

   3

   4

5   Which of the following establishments may use cafeteria service?
    ☐ works canteen   ☐ first class hotel
    ☐ popular restaurant   ☐ hostel

6   Name the type of service where customers usually help themselves
    to the food.

7   Give four advantages of automatic vending:
    1   2

    3   4

8   State four examples of different foods served at speciality
    restaurants.
    1   2

    3   4

16

The use of computers

pages 414–424

1 What is a *CPU*, and of what is it composed?

2 What do the following abbreviations stand for?

   IT

   DPU

3 What is the task of the catering manager if he is to make faster and more accurate decisions within the establishment?

4 State two functions of the computer that can help in achieving this aim:

   1

   2

5 What is the name given to the information stored by the computer?

   ☐ dictum   ☐ datum
   ☐ datsun   ☐ data

6 What is the name given to information processed by the computer?

7 What is the name given to the manufactured equipment we know as a computer?

☐ hardstore   ☐ hardware
☐ hardstock   ☐ hardstack

8 Instructions to computers are on tapes which are known as software: true/false.

9 The television screen with a keyboard like a typewriter is often the most distinctive feature of the computer and is known as a VDU. What do the letters stand for?

10 An important part of some printers is the daisy wheel. What is the function of the daisy wheel?

11 What is meant by a *recipe explosion*?

12 Which is the smaller the minicomputer or the microcomputer?

17

Industrial relations

pages 425–431

1   Effective relationships in industry depend upon

    1 cooperation between _____ and _____

    2 knowing _____ passed by Parliament

    3 having the _____ towards the laws

2   List six reasons why good industrial relations are not easy to create in the catering industry.

    1

    2

    3

    4

    5

    6

3   Very briefly state the purpose of a trade union.

4   What function should the shop steward perform?

5 What should the Sex Discrimination Act prevent?

6 Who does the Race Relation Act help?

7 What is the meaning of the word *discrimination*?

8 The Equal Pay Act specifies that equal pay is paid to whom?

9 When assessing people for employment what considerations must not affect the issue?

10 The Employment Act is concerned, among other things, with the dismissal of staff. Give two fair and two unfair grounds for dismissal.

Fair

1

2

Unfair

1

2

11 What do the following initials stand for?

AGM

AOB

12 What is an *agenda*?

13 A written record of committee decisions is termed

14 Why would a person be *out of order*.

15 Briefly explain:

ex officio   *status quo*

quorum

16 When all present at a meeting vote for the motion it is said to be

_____.

17 A vote in favour of a motion is said to be _____.

18

Guide to study and employment

pages 432–439

1   What is the name of the comprehensive record an employee or potential employee may send to an employer?

2   When applying for a job, the names of two people may be required to act as:

☐ umpires
☐ referees
☐ judges

3   State six qualities an employer may look for in a good prospective employee:

1   2

3   4

5   6

4   In which publication may you find advertisements for jobs in the catering industry?

5   What must never be written on a job application?

6 Which of the following should you take when going for an interview?

☐ any certificates you possess
☐ your mother, or close relative
☐ the address of where the interview is to be held
☐ the phone number of the potential employer
☐ any questions you may wish to ask
☐ a bottle of wine as a gift

7 At an interview which is the most important?

☐ to be clean, neat and to sit up and not smoke
☐ to be clean, neat but if nervous to ask for a light for a cigarette
☐ to lounge but be clean and tidy
☐ to be over-confident, ask many questions, be clean

8 Should you not obtain the job, state four reasons why you may have been rejected.

1

2

3

4

9 Besides money, what do you want from employment in the catering industry?

10 How may you remedy any shortcoming regarding your own employability?

Humorous and other questions

(*Answers on pages 155–158*)

Humorous

1   Would melted butter be served with silver fish?

2   On being told to draw the chicken would you use pen or pencil?

3   Would fans in the kitchen be Chelsea or Manchester United supporters?

4   Is a U bend a road sign in the kitchen?

5   Which garden would Basil and Rosemary have time to go and meet the sage in?

6   Would John Dory be suitable as the fish cook?

7   Is a salamander kept in the kitchen to catch insects?

8   Would you expect the governor to be in the chef's office?

9   If ox tongues are to be found in the larder, where would you find cats' tongues?

10 Sausage meat is rolled in puff pastry, what is rolled in a blanket?

11 Would you expect chillies to feel the cold?

151

12 Why might the skate want to fly?

13 When stock-taking, would the storekeeper take fish stock or brown stock?

14 Is it true that the still room at breakfast time is a peaceful place?

15 Which chef de partie has most cause to grumble after 12th August?

16 Could a culinary symphony be composed using triangles, mandolins, pipes, drums and horns?

17 If you were 'knocking it back' in the pastry would you be having a pint?

18 Would China or Indian tea be made with water from the fish kettle?

19 Could you end up in court with the copper?

20 Would you expect to find a seal in or under the sink?

American culinary terms

What are the English equivalents of these American culinary terms?

1 cookies

2 white raisins

3 granulated sugar

4 confectioner's sugar

5 zucchini

6 dry goods store

7 candy

8 faucet

9   molasses

10   tenderloin

11   corn starch

12   heavy cream

Culinary London (Cockney) rhyming slang

If a Cockney used the following culinary terms, to what would he/she be referring?

1   apples and pears

2   pig's ear

3   birdlime

4   pot and pan

5   tea-leaf

6   bangers and mash

7   frog and toad

8   rub-a-dub

9   plates of meat

10   mince pies

Initials and abbreviations

These initials and abbreviations are frequently used in the catering industry. What do they stand for?

1   EHO

2   ICA

3 MC

4 °F

5 CEMA

6 HASAW

7 oz

8 °C

9 EEC

10 CORGI

11 NICEIC

12 vit

13 HCIMA

14 CV

15 kg

16 WC

17 HMSO

18 kJ

19 C&GLI

20 veg

21 g

22 UK

23 VDU

Answers to humorous and other questions

Humorous

1   Not likely! Silver fish are very small insects found in very damp places.

2   Neither; you would take out the chicken innards.

3   More likely, extractor fans for ventilation. (Some of the staff could be supporters of these clubs.)

4   No, it is a bend in the pipe under the sink.

5   The herb garden – Basil, Rosemary, Thyme (pronounced 'time') and Sage are all herbs.

6   He could be, but John Dory is the name of a fish with thumb marks.

7   Most unlikely, lizards are not kept in kitchens. This salamander is for grilling goods.

8   You might, but a governor is fitted to most gas catering appliances.

9   In the pastry, *langues de chats* (cats' tongues) are a type of biscuit.

10   Any person unlucky enough to have their clothing on fire.

11   Not really since they are a type of mildly hot pepper.

12   Because it's got 'wings'!

13   Neither, he would take a list of the contents of the store.

14   No, because it's not still then; it's the still room's busiest time.

15   The roast cook, because grouse are now in season.

16   Maybe, triangles are used as pot stands, mandolins for slicing, pipes for piping, drums for salt and horns for cream horns.

17   More likely to be kneading or working the yeast dough.

18   Neither, only fish are cooked in fish kettles.

19   Only if you stole it! You are likely to use the copper on the stove.

20   Under the sink, it's the water in the U-bend which forms a seal.

American culinary terms

1	cookies	biscuits
2	white raisins	sultanas
3	granulated sugar	caster sugar
4	confectioner's sugar	icing sugar
5	zucchini	courgettes
6	dry goods store	drapers
7	candy	sweets
8	faucet	tap
9	molasses	treacle
10	tenderloin	fillet of beef
11	corn starch	corn flour
12	heavy cream	double cream

Culinary London (Cockney) rhyming slang

1	apples and pears	stairs
2	pig's ear	beer
3	birdlime	time
4	pot and pan	husband (old man)
5	tea-leaf	thief
6	bangers and mash	cash
7	frog and toad	road
8	rub-a-dub	pub
9	plates of meat	feet
10	mince pies	eyes

Initials and abbreviations

1	EHO	Environmental Health Officer
2	ICA	Industrial Caterers' Association
3	MC	Master of Ceremonies
4	°F	degrees Fahrenheit
5	CEMA	Catering Equipment Manufacturers' Association
6	HASWA	Health and Safety at Work Act
7	oz	ounce
8	°C	degrees Centigrade
9	EEC	European Economic Community
10	CORGI	Confederation for the Registration of Gas Installers

11	NICEIC	National Inspection Council for Electrical Contracting
12	vit	vitamin
13	HCIMA	Hotel Catering and Institutional Management Association
14	CV	Curriculum Vitae
15	kg	kilogram
16	WC	water-closet
17	HMSO	Her Majesty's Stationery Office
18	kJ	kilojoule
19	C&GLI	City and Guilds of London Institute
20	veg	vegetable
21	g	gram
22	UK	United Kingdom
23	VDU	Visual Display Unit

Answers to diagram questions

p 26 **35** No 2

p 36 **33** A: Brill   B: Turbot

p 38 **59** A: Crab   B: Lobster   C: Prawn   D: Shrimp
E: Scallop

p 39 **61** A: Crayfish   B: Crawfish

p 47 **32** A: Pear – William, Comice, Conference
B: Apple – Worcester pearmain, Cox's orange pippin,
Bramley
C: Melon – Honeydew, Canteloupe, Charentais

p 48 **9** 1: Walnut   2: Brazil   3: Almond   4: Coconut   5: Chestnut

p 56 **19** 1: Edam   2: Camembert   3: Brie   4: Gruyère

p 63 **4** 1: Jug   2: Cona   3: Saucepan   4: Expresso
5: Still set

p 79 **16** Unit   Min   Stock

p 79 **17** Invoice or Reg No   Received   Issued   Received

p 80 **21** Date   Description   Unit   Quan   Price per Unit p 82 **46**

	Monday Out	Wednesday In	Thursday Out
Butter	2	0	3
Flour	1	1	0
Olive Oil	1	0	$\frac{1}{2}$
Spices	4	8	0
Peas	6	0	3

p 85 **15** 1: Deep fat fryer   2: High pressure steamer   3: Bratt pan
4: Boiler pan   5: Steamer

p 89 **51** 1: Braising pan   2: Sauté pan   3: Sauteuse
4: Salmon kettle

p 90 **63** Friture: iron   Conical strainer: tinned steel
Musroon: wood   Sugar boiler: copper

p 91 **1** A: Radiation   B: Conduction   C: Convection

p 93 **6** 8612

p 96 **6** A: Side of cistern   B: Washer   C: Piston   D: Cap end
E: Split pin   F: Lever arm   G: Cold water inlet

p 109 **41** Air

p 109 **47** A

p 112 **8** Hair long and uncovered; scratching hair over food, thus
risking possibility of dandruff and/or loose hair falling into
food

p 113 **15** Mouth; nostrils; ears

p 114 **20** Apron too short; sleeves rolled up; high-heeled shoes;
wearing watch and ring; hair too long and not protected

p 115 **25** Long unprotected hair; smoking over food

p 119 **13** Port pie; trifle

p 120 **26** Chicken being drawn on same board as cooked meat being
sliced – risk of infection

p 121 **30** Salmonella

p 122 **39** Bird's nest; rats; swill uncovered; flies; fish and bread on same table; WC door open to kitchen

p 127 **21** Onion, because its main purpose is to provide flavour

p 128 **28** Blackcurrants, because they do not contain fat

p 130 **43** Oily fish, because it is the only food containing vitamin D